Collins

AQA GCSE (9–1)
Physics

Grade 5 Booster Workbook

For Combined Science: Trilogy

Stephanie Grant
Lynn Pharaoh

HarperCollins Publishers
The News Building
1 London Bridge Street
London SE1 9GF

HarperCollins *Publishers*
Macken House, 39/40,
Mayor Street Upper,
Dublin1 ,D01 C9W8

**Browse the complete Collins catalogue at
www.collins.co.uk**

10 9 8 7 6 5

© HarperCollins Publishers 2018

ISBN 978-0-00-829655-1

Collins® is a registered trademark of HarperCollins Publishers Limited

www.collins.co.uk

A catalogue record for this book is available from the British Library

Commissioned by Joanna Ramsay and Rachael Harrison
Development edited by Gillian Lindsey
Project managed by Sarah Thomas, Siobhan Brown and Mike Appleton
Copy edited by Gwynneth Drabble and Aidan Gill
Proofread by David Hemsley
Typeset by Jouve India Pvt Ltd.,
Cover design by We are Laura and Jouve
Cover image: Arsenis Spyros/Shutterstock, TaraPatta/Shutterstock
Production by Tina Paul
Printed by Ashford Colour Press Ltd.

This book contains FSC™ certified paper and other controlled sources to ensure responsible forest management.

For more information visit: www.harpercollins.co.uk/green

Contents

Introduction

This workbook will help you build your confidence in answering Physics questions for GCSE Combined Science.

It gives you practice in using key scientific words, writing longer answers, answering synoptic questions as well as applying knowledge and analysing information.

Learn how to answer test questions with annotated worked examples.

This will help you develop the skills you need to answer questions.

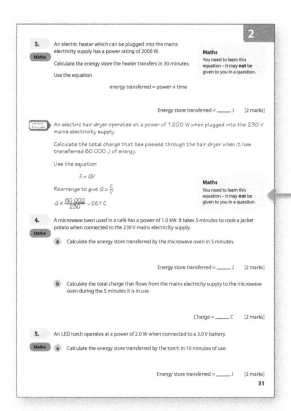

The amount of support gradually decreases throughout the workbook. As you build your skills you should be able to complete more of the questions yourself.

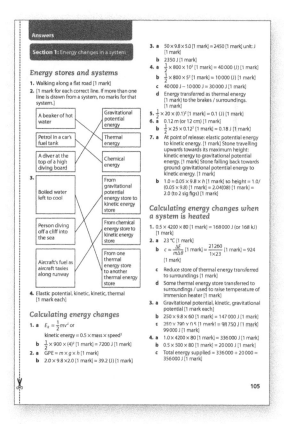

There are answers to all the questions at the back of the book. You can check your answers yourself or your teacher might tear them out and give them to you later to mark your work.

Energy stores and systems

1. Which movement does **not** change a person's store of gravitational potential energy?
Tick **one** box.

Riding a bicycle up a hill ☐

Running down the stairs ☐

Walking along a flat road ☐

Using a lift to change floor in a building ☐ [1 mark]

2. Draw **one** line from each system to its store of energy.

System	Store
A beaker of hot water	Gravitational potential energy
Petrol in a car's fuel tank	Thermal energy
A diver at the top of a high diving board	Chemical energy

[3 marks]

3. Draw **one** line from each system to the change in that system's energy store as time passes.

System	Change in energy stored
Boiled water left to cool	From gravitational potential energy store to kinetic energy store
Person diving off a cliff into the sea	From chemical energy store to kinetic energy store
Aircraft's fuel as aircraft taxies along runway	From one thermal energy store to another thermal energy store

[3 marks]

4. Complete the sentences about how the different energy stores change as a stone is fired at a wall from a catapult. Use words from the box.

thermal	kinetic	elastic potential

As the catapult is stretched, its store of _____

energy is increased. As the catapult is fired this store of energy is transferred to the

_____ energy store of the stone. As the stone hits the wall,

the _____ energy store of the stone decreases and the

_____ energy store of the wall increases. [4 marks]

Calculating energy changes

1. **a** Write down the equation which links speed, kinetic energy and mass.

Maths

_____ [1 mark]

> **Maths**
>
> You need to learn both these equations – they may **not** be given to you in a question.

b A car of mass 900 kg is travelling at 4 m/s.

Calculate the amount of kinetic energy it stores.

Kinetic energy store = _____ J [2 marks]

2. **a** Write down the equation which links gravitational field strength, gravitational potential energy, height and mass.

Maths

_____ [1 mark]

b A 2.0 kg box is lifted onto a 2.0 m high shelf. By how much does its gravitational potential energy change?

Gravitational field strength = 9.8 N/kg.

Change in store of gravitational potential energy = _____ J [2 marks]

3. **a** A diver of mass 50 kg stands on a 5.0 m high diving board.

Maths

Calculate the change in the diver's gravitational potential energy as she falls from the board into the water.

Give the unit for your answer.

Gravitational field strength = 9.8 N/kg.

Change in store of gravitational potential energy = _____

Unit _____ [2 marks]

b As the diver falls towards the swimming pool below, energy is transferred from a store of gravitational potential energy to a store of kinetic energy and the thermal energy store of the surrounding air.

If 100 J of her gravitational potential energy store is transferred to the thermal energy store of the air during the dive, how much kinetic energy does she have as she enters the water?

Kinetic energy store = _____ J   [1 mark]

4. **a** A car of mass 800 kg is travelling at 10 m/s. The driver applies the car's brakes, reducing the car's speed to 5 m/s.

Maths

Use the equation $E_k = \frac{1}{2}mv^2$ to calculate the car's initial store of kinetic energy.

Initial kinetic energy store = _____ J   [2 marks]

b Calculate the car's kinetic energy store when its speed has been reduced to 5 m/s.

Kinetic energy store = _____ J   [2 marks]

c Calculate the change in the car's kinetic energy store during the time the brakes are applied.

Change in store of kinetic energy = _____ J   [1 mark]

d Describe what happened to the kinetic energy store lost in part c.

_____

_____   [2 marks]

5. A spring has a spring constant of 20 N/m. It is extended by 0.1 m.

Maths By how much does its elastic potential energy change?

Use the equation $E_e = \frac{1}{2}ke^2$.

Change in store of elastic potential energy = _____ J [2 marks]

Remember
Although you are given the equation for elastic potential energy here, it is useful to understand what is meant by 'extension' and 'spring constant'. When a spring is stretched, the **increase** in its length is called the **extension**. A spring with a large value for 'k' is much harder to stretch than a spring with a small value for 'k'.

6. **a** The length of an unstretched spring is 0.020 m. The spring has a spring constant of 25 N/m. The spring is stretched so that its length is 0.140 m.

Calculate the spring's extension.

Extension = _____ m   [1 mark]

b Calculate the elastic potential energy stored in the stretched spring.

Elastic potential energy store = _____ J   [2 marks]

7. **a** A stone is fired vertically upwards using a catapult.

Maths

Describe the energy transfers that take place at the following points in the stone's path.

At the point of release:

_____

The stone is travelling upwards towards its maximum height:

_____

The stone is falling back towards the ground:

_____   [3 marks]

b The energy stored in the stretched catapult is 1.0 J. The mass of the stone in the catapult is 50 g. If all the elastic energy in the elastic potential energy store is transferred to the stone's gravitational potential energy store, calculate the height above the point of release the stone will reach.

Give your answer to two significant figures.

Gravitational field strength = 9.8 N/kg.

Maths

To **round** a number to two significant figures, look at the **third** digit. Round up if the digit is 5 or more, and round down if the digit is 4 or less.

For example, 1.62 rounds to 1.6.

Height = _____ m   [4 marks]

Calculating energy changes when a system is heated

1. Water has a specific heat capacity of 4200 J/kg °C. How much energy store is transferred to 500 g of water when its temperature increases from 20.0 °C to 100.0 °C?

Use the correct equation from the Physics Equation Sheet.

Maths

This question gives the mass in grams, so you first need to change the mass into kilograms.

Energy store transferred = _____ J   [2 marks]

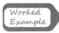

Worked Example

How much energy is needed to increase the temperature of 2.0 kg of water from 20 °C to 70 °C?

The specific heat capacity of water is 4200 J/kg °C.

The temperature change of the water, $\Delta\theta = 70° - 20° = 50$ °C

Energy needed = $mc\Delta\theta$

= 2.0 × 4200 × 50 = 420 000 J

2.

Practical

A student uses the apparatus shown in the diagram to measure the specific heat capacity of aluminium. A heater slots into the larger hole in the aluminium block and the thermometer slots in the smaller hole. The aluminium block is wrapped in expanded polystyrene, which is an insulator.

The joulemeter records the amount of energy transferred by the electric current to the thermal energy store of the immersion heater.

The student switches the power supply unit on for 10 minutes. The table shows the results.

Mass of block (kg)	Joulemeter reading (J)	Initial temperature of block (°C)	Temperature of block after heating (°C)
1.00	21 260	18.0	41.0

a Calculate the temperature rise of the block.

Temperature rise = _____ °C   [1 mark]

b Use the data in the table to calculate the specific heat capacity, *c*, of aluminium.

Use the correct equation from the Physics Equation Sheet.

Give your answer to three significant figures.

Specific heat capacity = _____ J/kg °C   [3 marks]

> **Maths**
>
> You will need to **rearrange** the equation for this calculation. This means putting specific heat capacity on its own, on one side of the equals sign.
>
> The equation is in the form $a = b \times c \times d$. To find *c*, divide both sides of the equation by *b*. Then divide both sides of the equation by *d*.

c Describe the purpose of the insulation wrapped around the aluminium block.

_____

_____ [1 mark]

d The accepted value for the specific heat capacity of aluminium is 910 J/kg °C.

Suggest a reason why the value obtained from the student's data is greater than the accepted value.

_____

_____ [1 mark]

3.

Maths

a A granite boulder of mass 250 kg falls from a cliff 60 m high to the ground below.

Complete the sentences to describe the energy transfers. Use words from the box.

thermal	gravitational potential	kinetic

At the top of the cliff, the boulder has a store of

_____ energy. As the boulder falls

its store of _____ energy increases and its store of

_____ decreases.   [3 marks]

boulder

60 m
cliff

b Calculate the change in the boulder's gravitational potential energy as it falls from the top of the cliff to the ground.

Gravitational field strength = 9.8 N/kg.

Change in store of gravitational potential energy = _____ J   [2 marks] c On striking the ground, the energy in the kinetic energy store of the boulder is transferred to the store of thermal energy of the boulder and the surrounding air. The temperature of the boulder increases by 0.5 °C.

Use the equation

change in thermal energy = mass × specific heat capacity × temperature change

to calculate the increase in the boulder's thermal energy store. Give your answer to two significant figures. The specific heat capacity of granite is 790 J/kg °C.

Increase in store of thermal energy = _____ J   [3 marks]

4. a An electric kettle contains 1.0 kg of water at 20 °C. The kettle is switched on until the water reaches 100 °C. Calculate the increase in the thermal energy store of the water.

The specific heat capacity of water is 4200 J/kg °C.

Maths

Maths

In an integer, zero is counted as a significant figure **only** if it is between two other non-zero significant digits. For example, the zeros in 10 000 are **not** significant.

Increase in thermal energy store of the water = _____ J   [2 marks]

b The kettle is made from stainless steel and has a mass of 0.50 kg. The temperature of the kettle is also increased from 20 °C to 100 °C. Calculate the increase in the thermal energy store of the kettle.

The specific heat capacity of stainless steel is 500 J/kg °C.

Increase in thermal energy of kettle = _____ J   [2 marks]

c Calculate the total energy store that would have to be supplied to the kettle from the electricity supply.

Total energy store supplied = _____ J   [1 mark]

Work and power

1. Work is done when a force moves an object from one place to another. When work is done, energy is transferred.

Draw **one** line to match each example of work to the energy transfer that takes place.

Maths

You need to learn the equations for work done and power – they may **not** be given to you in a question.

Example of work

The force of gravity pulling a free-wheeling cyclist faster and faster down a hill

A person pushing a heavy shopping trolley to get it moving

A person lifting a box from the floor onto a shelf

Energy transfer

From chemical energy store to kinetic energy store

From chemical energy store to gravitational potential energy store

From gravitational potential energy store to kinetic energy store

[3 marks]

2.

Synoptic

a A child pulling a sledge along a horizontal path exerts a force of 10 N for 10 s over a distance of 15 m.

Use the equation

$$\text{work done} = \text{force} \times \text{distance}$$

to calculate the work he does in pulling the sledge.

Synoptic

In the final exam, some of the marks will be for **connecting** your knowledge from different areas of physics. To answer this question you need to **link** knowledge of energy store transfer with ideas about forces (section 3).

Work done = _____ J   [2 marks]

b Use the equation

$$\text{power} = \frac{\text{work done}}{\text{time}}$$

to calculate the child's useful output power in moving the sledge.

Useful output power = _____ W   [2 marks]

3. **a** When a driver of a car applies the brakes, a force of 4000 N brings the car to a stop over a distance of 50 m.

Synoptic

Calculate the work done by the braking force.

Work done = _____ J   [2 marks]

b Calculate the braking power if the time taken to stop is 5.0 s.

Give your answer in kilowatts.

Braking power = _____ kW   [2 marks]

4. **a** An electric motor-driven crane lifts an 800 kg load a distance of 10 m. Calculate the gain in gravitational potential energy of the load.

Maths

Gravitational field strength = 9.8 N/kg.

Energy = _____ J   [2 marks]

b Calculate the useful power output of the crane if it takes 20 s to raise the load.

Useful power output = _____ W   [2 marks]

Conservation of energy

1. What name is given to the transfer of energy to a store from which it cannot be recovered? Tick **one** box.

Conduction ☐   Cooling ☐   Dissipation ☐   [1 mark]

2. Which one of the statements about energy is **incorrect**? Tick **one** box.

Energy can be usefully transferred from one energy store to another. ☐

Energy can be stored for future use. ☐

Energy can be destroyed. ☐

Energy can be dissipated. ☐   [1 mark]

3. A cyclist is travelling at a steady speed of 9 m/s along a flat road. The forces of friction and air resistance transfer 165 J of energy store away from the cyclist to the surroundings every second.

    How much useful output energy must the cyclist generate every second to maintain her steady speed?

    Useful output energy generated every second = _____ J   [1 mark]

4. A child is travelling at a steady speed along a horizontal path with a push scooter. When she stops pushing, the scooter gradually slows down and stops.

    Complete the sentences to explain what happens to the kinetic energy store of the scooter as it slows down.

    When the child stops pushing the kinetic energy store of the scooter

    _____.

    Energy is transferred away from the scooter because work is done by

    _____.

    The total energy store of the system (the child, the scooter and the surroundings) is

    _____.

    This means the energy in the kinetic energy store of the scooter has been transferred to

    _____.   [4 marks]

Ways of reducing unwanted energy transfers

1. Friction in the bearings of a bicycle wheel dissipates energy to the surroundings.

    How can this unwanted energy transfer can be reduced?

    _____   [1 mark]

2. When the heating in a house is switched off, the house cools down.

    Which changes could be made to the house so that it cools down more slowly?
    Tick **two** boxes.

    Increase the thermal conductivity of the walls   ☐

    Decrease the thermal conductivity of the walls   ☐

    Increase the thickness of the walls   ☐

    Decrease the thickness of the walls   ☐   [2 marks]

3. **a** The thermal energy lost from a house can be reduced by putting insulation on the floor of the loft.

The table shows three loft insulation materials and their thermal conductivity values.

Material	Thermal conductivity (W/m K)
cellulose	0.035
wool	0.038
polyurethane	0.024

Which material is the best insulator? Tick **one** box.

Cellulose   ☐

Wool   ☐

Polyurethane   ☐   [1 mark]

b Complete the sentences describing the effect of changing the thickness of the insulation in the loft of a house.

Use words from the box.

decreases   increases

Increasing the thickness of the insulation in the loft of a house _____ the rate of energy transfer by conduction through the insulation.

When the heating system in a house is switched off, the house cools down. Increasing the thickness of the loft insulation _____ the rate of cooling of the house.   [2 marks]

Efficiency

1. **a** Complete the sentences about energy changes in a car's diesel engine. Use words from the box.

thermal	kinetic	chemical

The diesel fuel in a car's fuel tank is a store of _____ energy. The car's

engine transfers energy from the store in the fuel to the _____ energy

store of the car. However some of the energy is dissipated to the surroundings, which

increases the _____ energy store of the surroundings. **[3 marks]**

b When the car's tank is full of diesel fuel it stores 1000 MJ of energy. When all the fuel has been used, the car's engine has transferred 420 MJ of this energy to the car to increase its store of kinetic energy. How much energy is dissipated to the surroundings?

Energy dissipated = _____ MJ **[1 mark]**

c Use the equation: $\text{efficiency} = \dfrac{\text{useful output energy transfer}}{\text{total input energy transfer}}$

to calculate the efficiency of the car's engine.

Give your answer as both a decimal and as a percentage.

> **Maths**
>
> You need to learn the equations for efficiency – they may **not** be given to you in a question.

Efficiency as a decimal = _____

Efficiency as a percentage = _____ % **[2 marks]**

2. A hybrid car has an efficiency of 80%.

Calculate the useful output energy if the engine is supplied with 500 MJ.

> **Maths**
>
> Efficiency values are often given as percentages. It is useful to remember that percentages are fractions of 100. So 40% is the fraction $\dfrac{40}{100}$.

Useful output energy = _____ MJ **[3 marks]**

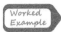

Worked Example The efficiency of car's diesel engine is 40%. Calculate the useful output energy if the total input energy of a tank of fuel is 1500 MJ.

40% as a fraction is $\frac{40}{100}$.

Substituting into the efficiency equation gives:

$\frac{40}{100} = \frac{\text{useful output energy transfer}}{1500}$.

So the useful output energy $= \frac{40}{100} \times 1500$

$$= 600 \text{ MJ}$$

3.

Maths

A gas-fired power station has an efficiency of 50%. How much input energy store must be transferred from the gas for every 1000 MJ of useful output electrical energy?

Input energy store = _____ MJ   [3 marks]

Maths
You will need to rearrange the equation to find the useful output energy. This means putting useful output energy on its own, on one side of the equals sign.

If an equation is given in the form $a = b/c$, to find b, first multiply both sides by c.

Maths
You could also work out the answer to this question using ratios. If the efficiency is 50%, only half of the input energy is usefully transferred so the input energy transfer must be twice as much as the useful output energy transfer.

Whichever method you use, always show how you work it out. Then you may still get some marks even if your final answer is wrong.

4.

Higher Tier only

The efficiency of a house heating system can be improved if less thermal energy is transferred from the house to the surrounding air.

Give **two** ways that this can be achieved.

_____

_____   [2 marks]

National and global energy resources

1. The percentage of the total energy used in generating electricity in the UK in 2013, 2014 and 2015 for the main four energy resources is shown in this table .

Energy resource	2013 total consumption (%)	2014 total consumption (%)	2015 total consumption (%)
coal	36	29.1	20.5
gas	27	30.2	30.2
nuclear	20	19.0	21.5
renewable	14.9	19.2	25.3

a Which **two** of the fuels in this table can be described as fossil fuels?

_____   [1 mark]

b Name a substance used as fuel in a nuclear power station.

_____   [1 mark]

c Coal, gas and nuclear are described as non-renewable energy resources.

Explain what is meant by a 'non-renewable energy resource'.

_____

_____   [2 marks]

d Describe the trends in the data shown in the table.

_____

_____

_____

_____   [3 marks]

Literacy

A **trend** is a pattern in data. Don't just say 'it goes up' or 'it goes down'. **Compare** the increase or decrease using data from the table.

e   Compare the environmental effects of using coal or nuclear fuel for generating electricity.

_____

_____

_____

_____ [3 marks]

Command words

A **compare** question means give similarities and differences. You will need to mention both parts in the comparison. Good words to use in your answers are 'both', 'however', 'whereas' and 'but'. Remember, 3 marks means 3 points are needed.

2.   In 2014, renewable energy sources provided 19.2% of the energy used for generating electricity in the UK. The four main types of renewable energy resource used in electricity generation in 2014 were onshore wind, offshore wind, solar panels (photovoltaic cells) and bio-fuel.

a   Give an example of a bio-fuel that can be used in the generation of electricity.

_____ [1 mark]

b   The reliability of power stations is measured by their ability to maintain a constant output of electricity.

Give **one** reason why it is important that the energy resources used to generate electricity are reliable.

_____

_____ [1 mark]

c   Describe the **problems** of reliability of wind power and solar (photovoltaic) panels as energy resources for generating electricity.

Wind power: _____

Solar power: _____ [2 marks]

3.   The graph compares the uses of energy in the UK by transport, homes and industry from 1970 to 2014. In the same period, the UK population increased from 55.7 million in 1970 to 64.6 million in 2014.

Compare the trends shown in this graph.

Million tonnes of oil equivalent (Mtoe)

■ Industry ▨ Domestic ■ Transport □ Other

Suggest possible explanations.

_____

_____

_____

_____

_____

_____

_____ [6 marks]

4. The UK uses less energy today than in 1970 even though the UK's population has increased by nearly 10 million. In the last 10 years, global energy consumption per person has increased by approximately 10%.

Suggest **two** reasons why the global trend in energy consumption is very different to that in the UK.

_____

_____ [2 marks]

Circuit diagrams

1. Draw **one** line from each circuit symbol to the correct description.

Symbol	Description

Symbol
+∣⊢
─o o─
─⊗─
─▭─

Description
open switch
cell
resistor
lamp

[4 marks]

2. A student is asked to build the circuit in the diagram. The components in the circuit are joined together using connecting leads. [1 mark]

What is the least number of connecting leads the student would need to build the circuit? Tick **one** box.

Three ☐   Four ☐   Five ☐   Six ☐   [1 mark]

3. Look at these four circuit diagrams labelled W, X, Y and Z.

circuit W

circuit X

a Which circuit contains a battery with two cells? Tick **one** box.

W ☐   X ☐

Y ☐   Z ☐   [1 mark]

circuit Y

circuit Z

b Which circuit does **not** contain a switch? Tick **one** box.

W ☐   X ☐   Y ☐   Z ☐   [1 mark]

c Which circuit contains an ammeter positioned to measure the electric current flowing through a resistor? Tick **one** box.

W ☐   X ☐   Y ☐   Z ☐   [1 mark]

d Which circuit contains the symbol for a closed switch? Tick **one** box.

W ☐   X ☐   Y ☐   Z ☐   [1 mark]

Electrical charge and current

1. This circuit diagram contains three ammeters, A1, A2 and A3.

   When the switch is closed, are the readings on ammeters A1, A2 and A3 the same or different?

   Give a reason for your answer.

   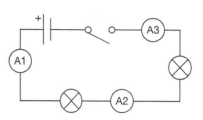

   _____

   _____ [2 marks]

2. A student builds the circuit shown in the diagram.

   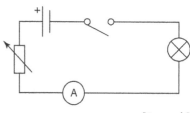

   a Complete the sentence.

   When the switch is closed, the ammeter

   measures the rate of flow of _____. [1 mark]

   b What is the source of potential difference in the circuit?

   _____ [1 mark]

   c Add a suitable meter to the circuit diagram that would enable the potential difference across the lamp to be measured. [2 marks]

   Maths
   You need to learn the equation for charge flow – it may **not** be given to you in a question.

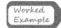

Calculate the current in a wire if a charge of 1.4 C flows through the wire in 4.0 s.

Use the equation

$$\text{charge flow} = \text{current} \times \text{time, or } Q = It$$

Rearrange the equation to make the current, I, the subject. Divide both sides of the equation by time, t.

$$I = \frac{Q}{t}$$

$$= \frac{1.4}{4.0} = 0.35 \text{ A}$$

d When the switch is closed, the ammeter reads 0.15 A.

Calculate the charge that flows through the lamp in 20 seconds.

Give the correct unit with your answer.

Electric current values are sometimes given in milliamps (mA). 'milli' is a prefix which means $\frac{1}{1000}$.

So 1 mA is equal to 0.001 A, which can also be written as 1×10^{-3} A.

Charge flow = _____ Unit: _____ [3 marks]

Maths **e** The variable resistor is now adjusted so that the lamp is much dimmer. The ammeter now reads 20 mA.

How much time does it take for 1.0 C of charge to flow through the lamp?

Time taken = _____ s [2 marks]

Electrical resistance

1. Draw **one** line from each quantity to its correct unit.

Quantity	Unit
Potential difference	ampere
Charge	volt
Current	ohm
Resistance	coulomb

[4 marks]

2. A student wants to measure the resistance of combinations of resistors. He has four identical resistors. Two resistors are connected in parallel and the other two in series.

Practical

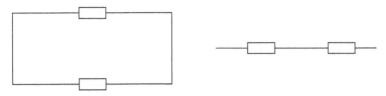

Add components to the circuit on the right to show how measurements can be made to determine the combined resistance of the two resistors in series. [3 marks]

3. When the switch in the circuit in this diagram is closed, the ammeter reads 0.25 A.

Maths **a** Resistor R has a resistance of 6.0 Ω.

The equation which links current, potential difference and resistance is:

potential difference = current × resistance

Maths

You need to learn this equation. It may **not** be given to you in a question.

Calculate the reading on the voltmeter when the switch is closed.

Voltmeter reading = _____ V   [2 marks]

b If resistor R was replaced with a resistor with a much bigger resistance, how would the ammeter reading change?

_____   [1 mark]

Maths **c** Resistor R is now replaced with a 1 metre length of nichrome wire. The voltmeter reads 1.5 V and the ammeter reads 48 mA.

What is the resistance of the wire?

Give your answer to two significant figures.

Remember

To round a number to two significant figures, look at the third digit. Round up if the digit is 5 or more, and round down if the digit is 4 or less.

Resistance of wire = _____ Ω   [3 marks]

4. A student plans an experiment to find out how the resistance of a piece of constantan wire depends on its length. She builds the circuit shown in the circuit diagram.

Practical

This is the student's plan:

- Attach crocodile clips to the wire.
- Measure the length of wire between the crocodile clips using a metre rule.
- Close the switch.
- Record the readings on the ammeter and voltmeter.
- Repeat the measurements for different lengths of wire.

a The student's measurements are shown in the table.

The resistance for the first set of measurements has already been calculated.

Complete the last column. Record the resistance values to the same number of decimal places as the first resistance value. **[3 marks]**

Length of wire (m)	Current (mA)	Potential difference (V)	Resistance of wire (Ω)
0.300	0.443	1.49	3.36336
0.400	0.333	1.49	
0.500	0.266	1.49	
0.600	0.222	1.49	
0.700	0.190	1.49	
0.800	0.166	1.49	
0.900	0.150	1.49	

Remember
To get the resistance in ohms, you need to convert the current values to amps.

b The student controlled the type of wire and potential difference across the ends of the wire.

Give **one other** variable that the student should have controlled in her investigation.

_____ **[1 mark]**

c Give **two** reasons why taking repeat readings for each length of wire would improve the experiment.

_____

_____ **[2 marks]**

d The student plots a line graph to analyse the measurements.

Which variable should go on each axis?

x-axis: _____

y-axis: _____ **[2 marks]**

Practical
When plotting a graph to analyse experiment measurements, the independent variable is usually plotted on the *x*-axis.

e To prevent the wire from getting too hot, the student used only one cell in the circuit.

Suggest another way of making sure the wire does not get too hot.

_____ **[1 mark]**

Resistors and *I–V* characteristics

1. A student is given a resistor labelled 6.8 Ω. She is asked to build a circuit to test whether the resistance of the resistor remains 6.8 Ω as the current through it is changed.

She is given this incomplete circuit diagram. The diagram has a component missing between points X and Y.

a Name a component that the student can adjust to vary the size of the current in the circuit.

_____ [1 mark]

b Complete the circuit diagram above to show the correct circuit diagram symbol for this component, between points X and Y. [1 mark]

c The student made a series of current and potential difference measurements for the 6.8 Ω resistor. She then plotted this graph of current against potential difference.

What change would she have made to the circuit to obtain the negative current and potential difference values?

_____

_____ [1 mark]

d What does the graph show about the relationship between the current and the potential difference?

Explain your answer.

_____

_____

_____ [3 marks]

2. **a** Complete the sentence. Use words from the box.

| potential difference | resistance | charge | temperature |

A component is described as an ohmic conductor if its _____

stays constant as the current through it is changed, at constant

_____. [2 marks]

b This is a graph of current against voltage for a diode. The graph shows that current flows through the diode in one direction only.

What is the relationship between the current and the potential difference in this graph? Tick **one** box.

Directly proportional ☐   Non-linear ☐

Inversely proportional ☐   [1 mark]

c Describe the resistance of the diode in the reverse direction.

_____ [1 mark]

3.

Practical

A box labelled X contains a mystery electrical component. A student is asked to investigate the relationship between the current through the component and the potential difference applied across it.

Design a method the student could use to investigate the relationship between the current and potential difference for the mystery component.

Include in your description the measurements she should make and how she should obtain negative values.

A circuit diagram may be drawn as part of your answer.

Practical

When the question asks you to **design** an experiment, you need to set out the steps – how the experiment will be done. Picture yourself doing the experiment so that the instructions will be clear to someone else even if they have not done a similar experiment before.

_____

_____

_____

_____ [6 marks]

4. This circuit contains a light-dependent resistor (LDR).

a What quantity does the voltmeter measure?

_____ [1 mark]

Maths **b** When the switch is closed the meter readings are taken. The ammeter reads 3.52 mA and the voltmeter reads 1.51 V.

Calculate the resistance of the LDR.

Resistance = _____ Ω   [2 marks]

Maths **c** The LDR is now covered with a black cloth that stops any light from hitting the LDR. The ammeter now reads 1.23 mA and the voltmeter reads 1.51 V.

Calculate the new resistance of the LDR.

Resistance = _____ Ω   [2 marks]

d What can you conclude about how the resistance of an LDR can be changed?

_____

_____   [2 marks]

5. This diagram shows an ohmmeter used to measure the resistance of an electrical component.

a A student is asked to measure the resistance of a thermistor using an ohmmeter.

Complete the circuit diagram to show the thermistor connected between points X and Y.   [1 mark]

b The thermistor is placed in a beaker of hot water to change its temperature. The resistance of the thermistor is measured as the water cools down. The water temperature is measured with a thermometer.

Thermistor resistance versus temperature

The student plots a graph of resistance against temperature.

What can you conclude from this graph about how the resistance of a thermistor can be changed?

_____

_____   [2 marks]

Series and parallel circuits

1. **a** This circuit diagram contains three identical resistors.

Which statements about the circuit are true?
Tick **two** boxes.

The resistors are in series. ☐

Each resistor has a different current through it. ☐

The same current flows through all three resistors. ☐

The resistors are in parallel. ☐   [2 marks]

Maths **b** Each of the resistors has a resistance of 2.2 Ω.

What is the equivalent resistance of the three resistors in this circuit?

Equivalent resistance = _____ Ω   [1 mark]

Maths **c** The potential difference across the cell is 1.5 V.

What will be the potential difference across one of the 2.2 Ω resistors when the switch is closed?

Potential difference = _____ V   [1 mark]

2. Three different resistors are connected to a cell as shown in the circuit diagram.

a Which statements apply to the circuit?
Tick **two** boxes.

The resistors are in series. ☐

Each resistor has a different potential difference across it. ☐

The three resistors have the same potential difference across them. ☐

The resistors are in parallel. ☐   [2 marks]

Maths **b** The potential difference across the cell is 1.5 V.

Calculate the current through the 5 Ω resistor.

Current = _____ A   [2 marks]

3. In this circuit diagram, the potential difference across the cell is 1.5 V.

Maths

a Calculate the current flowing through the ammeter when switch X is open.

Current = _____ A   [2 marks]

b Calculate the current flowing through the ammeter when switch X is closed.

Current = _____ A   [2 marks]

Mains electricity

1. **a** What is the frequency of the mains electricity supply in the UK?

_____   [1 mark]

b What is the potential difference of the mains electricity supply in the UK?

_____   [1 mark]

2. Draw **one** line from each wire in a mains electricity cable to the job that it does.

> **Common misconception**
>
> Electricity is not an energy store, but a way of transferring energy from one store to another.

Wire	Job done
Neutral	Carries the alternating potential difference from the supply
Live	Acts as a safety device
Earth	Completes the circuit

[3 marks]

3. Complete the sentences to describe the mains electricity supply in the UK. Use words from the box.

direct   live   earth   alternating   blue   brown   neutral

The potential difference of the UK mains electricity supply is _____.

The live wire in the mains cable is coloured _____.

If the appliance becomes faulty, the _____ wire prevents the person using

the appliance from receiving an electric shock.   [3 marks]

4. An electric kettle can develop a fault in which the outer metal casing becomes connected to the live wire inside the kettle.

Explain how the earth wire prevents anyone who touches the kettle from getting an electric shock.

_____

_____

_____   [3 marks]

Command words

There are three marks here so make three points. Remember that '**explain**' means you have to say **what** happens and also **why** it happens.

Energy changes in circuits

1. Complete the sentences to describe the energy transferred by the appliances. Choose your answers from the box.

thermal	gravitational potential	kinetic

A food mixer transfers energy from the mains electricity supply to _____

energy. The current in an electric kettle transfers energy to water as _____

energy.   [2 marks]

2. A vacuum cleaner transfers energy from the mains electricity supply to air, increasing its store of kinetic energy.

Which changes would result in a bigger transfer of energy by a vacuum cleaner?
Tick **two** boxes.

Operate the vacuum cleaner for a longer period of time   ☐

Operate the vacuum cleaner for a shorter period of time   ☐

Use a vacuum cleaner with a lower power rating   ☐

Use a vacuum cleaner with a higher power rating   ☐   [2 marks]

3.

Maths

An electric heater which can be plugged into the mains electricity supply has a power rating of 2000 W.

Calculate the energy store the heater transfers in 30 minutes.

Use the equation

$$\text{energy transferred} = \text{power} \times \text{time}$$

Maths

You need to learn this equation – it may **not** be given to you in a question.

Energy store transferred = _____ J   [2 marks]

Worked Example

An electric hair dryer operates at a power of 1200 W when plugged into the 230 V mains electricity supply.

Calculate the total charge that has passed through the hair dryer when it has transferred 60 000 J of energy.

Use the equation

$$E = QV$$

Rearrange to give $Q = \dfrac{E}{V}$

$$Q = \frac{60\,000}{230} = 261\,C$$

Maths

You need to learn this equation – it may **not** be given to you in a question.

4.

Maths

A microwave oven used in a café has a power of 1.0 kW. It takes 5 minutes to cook a jacket potato when connected to the 230 V mains electricity supply.

a Calculate the energy store transferred by the microwave oven in 5 minutes.

Energy store transferred = _____ J   [2 marks]

b Calculate the total charge that flows from the mains electricity supply to the microwave oven during the 5 minutes it is in use.

Charge = _____ C   [2 marks]

5.

Maths

An LED torch operates at a power of 2.0 W when connected to a 3.0 V battery.

a Calculate the energy store transferred by the torch in 10 minutes of use.

Energy store transferred = _____ J   [2 marks]

b Calculate the total charge that flows through the torch in 10 minutes of use.

Charge = _____ C   [2 marks]

Electrical power

1.

Maths

Calculate the power of an electric food mixer that carries a current of 2.0 A when plugged into the 230 V mains electricity supply.

Maths
You need to learn this equation – it may **not** be given to you in a question.

Use the equation

power = potential difference × current

Give the correct unit for your answer.

Power = _____ Unit: _____   [2 marks]

Worked Example

The current in a resistor transfers energy to the resistor as thermal energy. The resistor gets hot.

Calculate the energy transferred by second by a 6.0 Ω resistor if it was carrying a current of 80.0 mA.

Power, $P = I^2R$

   $= 0.08^2 \times 6.0 = 0.49$ W

2.

Maths

A 30.0 m long extension cable has a resistance of 0.40 Ω.

Calculate the power loss in the extension cable when it is carrying a current of 4.0 A.

Power loss = _____ W   [3 marks]

3.

Maths

Microwave oven A draws a current of 2.6 A when connected to the 230 V mains electricity supply. Microwave B draws a current of 3.9 A when connected to the 230 V mains electricity supply.

Explain why microwave B cooks food more quickly than microwave A.

_____

_____

_____ [3 marks]

4. An electrical heater for a fish tank draws a current of 0.40 A when connected to the 230 V mains electricity supply.

Maths

a Calculate the power of the heater.

Power = _____ W [2 marks]

b Calculate the energy transferred by the heater when it is switched on for 10 minutes.

Energy transferred = _____ J [2 marks]

The National Grid

1. The National Grid system delivers electricity generated at power stations to towns and cities all over the country.

Give **one** reason why the National Grid system is better than each town having its own power station.

_____

_____ [1 mark]

2. Complete the sentences about transformers. Choose your answers from the box.

increases	decreases

A step-up transformer _____ the potential difference and

_____ the current. A step-down transformer _____ the

potential difference and _____ the current. [4 marks]

3. In the diagram, the cables shown as lines are part of the National Grid system. Transformer A is connected between the power station and the National Grid. Transformer B is connected between the National Grid and a school.

| power station | — | transformer A | — cables — | transformer B | — | school |

Which is the correct description of transformers A and B? Tick **one** box.

Synoptic

More information about how transformers work is included in the Higher Tier work in section 7.

Transformer A is a step-down and transformer B is a step-up. ☐

Transformer A and transformer B are both step-up. ☐

Transformer A is a step-up and transformer B is a step-down. ☐

[1 mark]

4. Which two statements about the National Grid are correct? Tick **two** boxes.

The National Grid transmits electricity at high voltages to improve efficiency. ☐

The National Grid transmits electricity at low voltages to improve efficiency. ☐

The National Grid transmits electricity at high currents to improve efficiency. ☐

The National Grid transmits electricity at low currents to improve efficiency. ☐

[2 marks]

5. When you boil water in an electric kettle the kettle draws electric current from the National Grid.

Which **one** of the following is **not** a part of the National Grid?

Kettle cable ☐

Overhead transmission cables ☐

Step-down transformer ☐

Step-up transformer ☐

[1 mark]

Density

1. Write down the equation which links density, mass and volume.

_____ [1 mark]

Maths

You need to learn this equation – it may not be given to you in a question.

Worked Example

Calculate the mass of an object with a density of 2 kg/m³ and volume of 3 m³.

Use the equation $density = \frac{mass}{volume}$

Rearrange the equation to make mass the subject.

mass = density × volume

$= 2 \text{ kg/m}^3 \times 3 \text{ m}^3$

$= 6 \text{ kg}$

2. A wooden object has a density of 740 kg/m³. Its mass is 3700 g.

Maths

Calculate the object's volume.

Give the unit.

Volume = _____ Unit _____ [4 marks]

Maths

In this example you'll need to rearrange the equation to find the mass. This means putting mass on its own, on one side of the equals sign.

This equation is given in the form $a = b/c$. To find b, multiply both sides by c.

Maths

Be careful of units when you substitute values into an equation. The unit of mass needs to match the unit of density. There are 1000 g in 1 kg.

3. **a** Which apparatus would be best for measuring a length less than 5 mm in size? Tick **one** box.

Practical

Metre ruler ☐   Micrometer ☐   30 cm ruler ☐   [1 mark]

b Which apparatus is used for measuring the volume of a liquid? Tick **one** box.

Measuring cylinder ☐   Displacement can ☐   30 cm ruler ☐   [1 mark]

4.

Practical

a A scientist finds a rock they believe to be a small meteorite. The rock has an **irregular** shape.

Describe a method the scientist could use to calculate the density of the rock.

Your answer should consider possible sources of error and how these could avoided.

_____

_____

_____

_____

_____

_____

_____ **[6 marks]**

Maths **b** Most meteorites have a density greater than most terrestrial (Earth) rocks.

Density of meteorites: 3000 to 8000 kg/m³

Density of terrestrial rocks: 2500 to 3200 kg/m³

The mass of the rock is found to be 0.112 kg and the volume is 0.000 031 m³.

Show that the rock is probably a meteorite.

_____

_____

_____

_____ **[4 marks]**

5. Describe a method you could use to find the density of an unknown liquid in the laboratory.

Higher Tier only

Synoptic

_____

_____

_____

_____

_____

_____

_____

Synoptic

In the final exam some of the marks will be for connecting your knowledge from different areas of physics. To answer this question you need to link knowledge of the particle model with ideas about upthrust (section 5).

[4 marks]

The diagram shows the arrangement of particles in a liquid. Each circle represents one particle.

a Draw a diagram in the box to show the arrangement of particles in a gas.

[2 marks]

b Use the diagrams to explain why gas bubbles accelerate upwards in fizzy drinks.

_____

_____

_____ [3 marks]

1. **a** Draw **one** line to match each change of state with its description. [4 marks]

Change of state	Description
Freeze	gas changes to liquid
Boil	solid changes to liquid
Condense	liquid changes to gas
Melt	liquid changes to solid

b For which **two** changes of state does energy needs to be **supplied**?

_____

_____ [2 marks]

2. Iodine is a material which sublimates.

What is meant by 'sublimates'?

_____ [1 mark]

3. What makes freezing a **physical** (**not** chemical) change?

_____ [1 mark]

4. Which one of the following is **not** a physical change? Tick **one** box.

Sublimation ☐   Burning ☐   Evaporating ☐ [1 mark]

5. A liquid is poured into a tray and then frozen.

Student A thinks that the mass of the frozen solid will be greater than the mass of the liquid.

Student B thinks that the masses will be the same.

Who do you agree with?

Explain your answer.

_____

_____ [2 marks]

Specific heat capacity and latent heat

1. Describe the movement of the particles in a hot gas compared to a cold gas.

_____ [1 mark]

2. When a gas is heated, which energy store in the gas increases? Tick **one** box.

Kinetic energy ☐   Gravitational potential energy ☐   Elastic energy ☐   [1 mark]

3. There is a bath of luke-warm water next to a cup of hot coffee.

a The coffee has a higher temperature. What does this tell you about the particles it contains?

_____ [1 mark]

b The water in the bath has a greater store of internal energy than the coffee in the cup.

Explain why, in terms of the particles it contains.

_____

_____ [2 marks]

4. 1 kg of ice at 0 °C has less internal energy than 1 kg of water at 0 °C. Explain why.

_____

_____ [2 marks]

5. A block of ice is heated for a few minutes. Even though thermal energy is still being supplied, the temperature of the ice and the melted water does not increase. Explain why.

_____

_____ [2 marks]

6. Look at the graph.

Graph to show how temperature varies with time for a solid being heated

a Label the following regions on the graph: **melting, liquid, boiling, solid**. [4 marks]

b Which of these regions does the term **specific latent heat of fusion** relate to?

_____ [1 mark]

Maths **c** The specific latent heat of fusion for this material is 45 kJ/kg.

Calculate the energy required to change 5 kg of the material from a solid to a liquid.

Use the equation

energy for a change of state = mass × specific latent heat

Maths

This equation is provided in the Physics Equation Sheet. You should be able to select and apply the equation – it may **not** be given in the question.

Energy = _____ J [2 marks]

7. A 500 g sample of a material is found to require 15 000 J to melt.

Calculate the specific latent heat of fusion for this material.

Use the correct equation from the Physics Equation Sheet.

Maths

You will need to select the correct equation, then rearrange the equation to give specific latent heat as the subject. Try dividing both sides of the equation by mass.

Specific latent heat of fusion = _____ J/kg [3 marks]

Particle motion in gases

1. Why does a gas exert pressure on its container?

_____ [1 mark]

2. What changes about the particles in a gas when the temperature is increased?

_____ [1 mark]

3. The temperature of a gas in a container of fixed volume is increased.

Explain what will happen to the pressure.

_____

_____

_____ [3 marks]

> **Command word**
>
> 'Explain' means you have to say **what** happens and also **why** it happens. There are 3 marks here so make **three** points.

4. It is dangerous to heat a sealed conical flask over a Bunsen burner.

Synoptic

   a Describe **one** possible dangerous outcome.

_____ [1 mark]

   b Explain your answer.

_____

_____ [2 marks]

5.

Synoptic

A cook pours hot jam into a jar. He immediately puts the lid on, leaving a layer of air above the jam's surface. After the jam has cooled, it becomes difficult to remove the lid.

Explain why.

_____

_____

_____

_____

_____ [4 marks]

6. Gas molecules move around at varying speeds in random directions.

A gas is kept at a constant temperature in a container which has a fixed volume.

Describe **two** things that can happen to a gas molecule in the container that could cause its speed or direction to change.

_____

_____

_____ [2 marks]

Protons, neutrons and electrons

1. Complete the table to describe the properties of protons, neutrons and electrons.

The electrons in an atom occupy different energy levels.

Particle	Charge	Mass	Located inside or outside nucleus?
	positive		
neutron			
		negligible	outside nucleus

[8 marks]

2. Complete the sentences.

The energy levels correspond to how far the electrons are from the _____.

Higher energy levels are _____ from the nucleus. Electrons can move

between energy levels – if an electron emits electromagnetic radiation it has moved to a

_____ energy level. [3 marks]

3. The Sun emits radiation at all wavelengths in the electromagnetic spectrum. To reach the surface of the Earth, this radiation must pass through the gases in the Sun's outer layers and the gases in the Earth's atmosphere.

Suggest what happens to atoms in these gases when radiation from the Sun passes through.

_____

_____ [2 marks]

The size of atoms

1. Put these powers of 10 in order of size from **smallest** to **largest**:

10^3	10^{-5}	10^1	10^4

Maths

Remember, a **negative** power of ten means a number **less than one**.

_____ [4 marks]

2.

Which one of these measurements is equivalent to 0.002 m?
Tick **one** box.

2×10^3 m ☐ 2×10^{-2} m ☐

2×10^2 m ☐ 2×10^{-3} m ☐   [1 mark]

3.   If the nucleus of an atom was the size of an apple, approximately what would the size of the whole atom be? Tick **one** box.

A plate ☐   An armchair ☐   A room ☐   A football pitch ☐   [1 mark]

4.   Look at the distances below.

A 1×10^{-10} m   C 1×10^{-14} m

B 1×10^{-6} m   D 1×10^{-20} m

Which is closest to:

a   The radius of an **atom**?

_____ [1 mark]

b   The radius of a **nucleus**?

_____ [1 mark]

Elements and isotopes

1.   Complete the sentences.

Use words from the box.

positive	negative	neutral	electrons
neutrons	protons	mass	atomic

Atoms have a _____ charge. Therefore the number of protons must

be equal to the number of _____. An element is defined by the

number of _____ in the nucleus. This is known as the element's

_____ number. The mass number is the sum of the number of

_____ and number of _____.   [6 marks]

2. Complete the table.

Atomic number of element	Mass number	Number of protons	Number of neutrons
	12	6	
11			12
	59		32
		13	14

Literacy

Two of these column headings basically mean the **same** thing. Which are they?

[8 marks]

3. Define an isotope.

_____

_____

_____ [3 marks]

4. An isotope of cobalt has a mass number of 60. The atomic number of cobalt is 27.

a Write down the number of protons, neutrons and electrons in an atom of this isotope.

Number of protons = _____

Number of neutrons = _____

Number of electrons = _____ [3 marks]

b The chemical symbol for cobalt is Co.

Write in symbol form how the nucleus of this isotope can be represented.

_____ [1 mark]

c Another isotope of cobalt has a mass number of 59.

Write in symbol form how the nucleus of this isotope can be represented.

_____ [1 mark]

Electrons and ions

1. Draw **one** line to match each statement on the left to the correct result on the right.

   Statement

   | Having a different number of neutrons in the nucleus |
   | Having a different number of electrons orbiting the nucleus |
   | Having a different number of protons in the nucleus |

   Results in

   | An ion of the same element |
   | A different element |
   | A different isotope of the same element |

   [3 marks]

2. An atom **loses** an electron.

   Is it now positively charged or negatively charged?

   Explain why.

   _____

   _____ [3 marks]

3. An atom of chlorine has a mass number of 35 and the atomic number is 17. The atom gains an electron to become an ion with a charge of −1.

   Give the number of protons, neutrons and electrons in the ion.

   Number of protons = _____

   Number of neutrons = _____

   Number of electrons = _____ [3 marks]

4. An atom of aluminium has a mass number of 27 and the atomic number is 13. The atom loses two electrons to become an ion with a charge of +2.

   Give the number of protons, neutrons and electrons in the ion.

   Number of protons = _____

   Number of neutrons = _____

   Number of electrons = _____ [3 marks]

Discovering the structure of the atom

1. The earliest idea about atoms was that atoms are the smallest particle.

   State the discovery which showed this theory to be incorrect.

   _____ [1 mark]

2. **a** Describe the plum pudding model of the atom.

   _____

   _____ [2 marks]

   b Which statement best describes where positive charge is located in the plum pudding model?

   Concentrated in a small space ☐   Spread out everywhere ☐   [1 mark]

3. Describe the differences between Rutherford's model of the atom and Niels Bohr's model of the atom.

   _____

   _____ [2 marks]

4. The alpha-scattering experiment showed that the nucleus was charged.

   State the **two** later discoveries that gave further information about the structure of the nucleus.

   _____

   _____ [2 marks]

5. Look at the diagram of the alpha-scattering experiment.

   a Label the grey box and gold square.   [2 marks]

b What results would be expected in this experiment if the plum-pudding model is correct?

Tick **one** box.

All the alpha particles would bounce back. ☐

All the alpha particles would go straight through. ☐

Some alpha particles would go through and others would bounce back. ☐

some alpha particles bounce back

fluorescent screen

most alpha particles hit here

some alpha particles are deflected

[1 mark]

c Describe the results actually obtained in the alpha-scattering experiment.

_____

_____ [2 marks]

6. Ernest Rutherford developed a new model of the atom from the results of the alpha-scattering experiment.

Describe the Rutherford model of the atom.

Explain how the results of the alpha-scattering experiment provided evidence for this model.

Literacy
To break this question down, take each result in turn and explain what it implies about the structure of the atom.

_____

_____

_____

_____

_____

_____

_____

_____ [6 marks]

Radioactive decay

1. Name the subatomic particle that is lost from an atom by beta decay.

_____ [1 mark]

2. Complete the sentences.

Nuclear radiation refers to radiation emitted from the _____ of an atom. This

process is known as radioactive decay and occurs when the nucleus is _____.

It is impossible to predict exactly when a nucleus will decay – it is a _____

process. The activity of a radioactive source is a measure of its rate at which the nuclei decay

and is measured in _____. Geiger–Muller tubes detect the number of decays

per second, which is known as the _____. [5 marks]

3. When an atom decays it emits one of four types of nuclear radiation: an alpha particle, a beta particle, a gamma ray or a neutron.

a In which type of radioactive decay is a neutral particle emitted?

_____ [1 mark]

b Which type of nuclear radiation consists of a high-speed electron?

_____ [1 mark]

c Which type of nuclear radiation is an electromagnetic wave?

_____ [1 mark]

d Describe the structure of an alpha particle.

_____

_____ [2 marks]

e Describe what happens when a radioactive nucleus emits a beta particle.

_____

_____ [2 marks]

Comparing alpha, beta and gamma radiation

1. Complete the table to compare the properties of alpha, beta and gamma radiation.

Type of radiation	Stopped by	Range in air
beta		
	several cm of lead	
		1–2 cm

[6 marks]

2. Alpha, beta and gamma radiation are all forms of **ionising** radiation.

   a What is meant by **ionising**?

   _____ [1 mark]

   b Which type of nuclear radiation is the most ionising?

   _____ [1 mark]

3. To diagnose problems with organs in the body, a radioactive tracer can be injected into a patient. The radiation emitted by the tracer is then detected outside the patient's body.

   Give **one** reason why a beta source is not suitable to use as a tracer in the body.

   _____ [1 mark]

4. Ionising radiation is used to kill cancerous cells.

   a Would you use an alpha or beta source to kill cancerous cells near the surface of the skin? Give a reason for your answer.

   _____

   _____

   _____ [1 mark]

   b Explain why gamma radiation is not suitable to use for treating skin cancer.

   _____

   _____ [2 marks]

5. One of the uses of nuclear radiation is to monitor the thickness of paper being produced in a factory.

Explain which of alpha, beta and gamma radiation you would choose for this application.

_____

_____

_____ [3 marks]

Radioactive decay equations

1. Which symbol correctly represents an alpha particle? Tick **one** box.

$^{4}_{4}\text{He}$ ☐ $^{4}_{0}\text{He}$ ☐ $^{4}_{2}\text{He}$ ☐ $^{2}_{2}\text{He}$ ☐   [1 mark]

> **Remember**
> To help you remember the symbol for an alpha particle, remember that the alpha particle is identical to a helium nucleus. The question is asking you to show the mass and atomic number for a helium nucleus.

2. Which symbol correctly represents a beta particle? Tick **one** box.

$^{1}_{0}\text{e}$ ☐ $^{0}_{1}\text{e}$ ☐ $^{0}_{-1}\text{e}$ ☐ $^{-1}_{-1}\text{e}$ ☐   [1 mark]

> **Remember**
> The fact an electron has a negative atomic number is a bit confusing! Remember that when a beta particle is emitted a neutron turns **into** a proton. The total atomic number must be the same before and after.

Worked Example

An atom of the isotope polonium-84 decays into an atom of lead-82.

State whether this is alpha or beta decay.

Complete the nuclear equation.

$$^{208}_{84}\text{Po} \rightarrow \underline{}^{}_{82}\text{Pb} + \underline{}$$ [2 marks]

The decay shows that two protons have been lost from the nucleus that decays. This must mean it is an alpha decay and so the missing particle on the right is $^{4}_{2}\text{He}$.

The mass numbers have to balance either side of the equation. An alpha particle has a mass number of 4 so the mass number of the lead (Pb) isotope must be equal to 208 − 4 = 204.

3. Complete the nuclear equation below to represent the beta decay of carbon-14.

$$^{14}_{6}C \rightarrow \underline{\quad}^{14}N + \underline{\quad} e$$

[2 marks]

4. An atom of thorium-90 decays into an atom of radon (Ra) by emitting an alpha particle.

Complete the nuclear equation below to represent the decay of thorium-90.

$$^{229}_{90}Th \rightarrow \underline{\quad}_{88}Ra + \underline{\quad}$$

[2 marks]

5. An atom of the isotope lead-82 decays into an atom of bismuth (Bi) by emitting a beta particle.

Complete the nuclear equation for this decay.

$$^{209}_{82}Pb \rightarrow \underline{\quad}Bi + beta\ particle$$

[2 marks]

6. An atom of cobalt-27 decays into an atom of nickel. Nickel has an atomic number of 28.

> **Remember**
>
> Both the mass numbers and the atomic numbers have to balance on both sides of the equation.

a What particle has been emitted by this radioactive decay?

_____ [1 mark]

b Complete the nuclear equation for this decay.

$$^{60}_{27}Co \rightarrow \underline{\quad}Ni + \underline{\quad}$$

[2 marks]

Half-lives

1. What is the half-life of a radioactive isotope? Tick **one** box.

The average time it takes for the mass of the sample to halve. ☐

The average time it takes for the activity of the sample to halve. ☐

The average time it takes for the mass number to halve. ☐ [1 mark]

> **Common misconception**
>
> Note that 'mass of the sample' is not the same as 'mass of the radioactive isotope'. When the isotope decays, it still has mass. So the **total** mass of the sample may **not change** very much, but the mass of the original radioactive isotope will decrease a lot.

2.

The graph shows the number of counts recorded per second from a sample of radioactive material.

a Use the graph to determine the half-life of this material.

Command words

The question asks you to **show** how you work out your answer from the graph. This means you must draw a line on the graph to show how you worked out your answer.

Show on the graph how you work out your answer.

_____ seconds   [2 marks]

b Determine how long it will it take for the count rate to reduce from its starting value of 400 counts per s to approximately 6 counts per s.

Maths

Try writing down 400 then drawing an arrow. Then write down the number which is half of 400. Then draw another arrow. Repeat this until you reach about 6. Then count the arrows and this is the number of times you have had to halve the initial count rate of 400 counts per s.

_____ seconds   [2 marks]

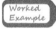

The initial activity of a radioactive isotope is 100 Bq and the half-life is 10 years. Determine how long it will it take for the activity to reduce to approximately 6 Bq.

$100 \rightarrow 50 \rightarrow 25 \rightarrow 12.5 \rightarrow 6.25$.

We have halved 100 four times here.

That means 4 half-lives will have passed. Four half-lives is 4×10 years = 40 years.

3. A Geiger–Muller tube records the number of radioactive decays per second.

Describe how you can be sure you are **only** counting the decays of the sample and not of other materials.

_____

_____   [2 marks]

The count rate of a radioactive source is recorded every minute. The background count is subtracted from each reading.

The table shows the results:

Time (minutes)	Count rate (counts per s)	Time (minutes)	Count rate (counts per s)
0	200	6	68
1	175	7	57
2	146	8	48
3	120	9	38
4	96	10	33
5	83	11	30

a Plot the results from the table on the graph. [2 marks]

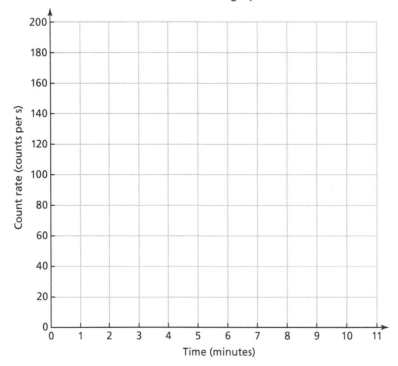

b Draw a line of best fit. [1 mark]

c Determine the time taken for the count rate to decrease from 200 to 100.

_____ minutes [1 mark]

d Determine the time taken for the count rate to decrease from 100 to 50.

_____ minutes [1 mark]

e   Estimate how long it would take for the count-rate to reduce to approximately 6 counts per s.

_____ minutes   [3 marks]

5.   The half-life of a radioactive substance is 6 hours.

Maths   Calculate how long it will take a sample of mass 0.64 g to decay until there is only 0.08 g of the original isotope.

_____ hours   [3 marks]

6.   10 g of a radioactive isotope decays until 1.25 g remains. The process takes 600 years.

Maths   Calculate the half-life of the material.

_____ hours   [3 marks]

Radioactive contamination

1.   Describe **two** precautions that someone could take to reduce the radiation hazard if they were handling:

a   A source of beta radiation

_____

_____   [2 marks]

b   A source of gamma radiation

_____

_____   [2 marks]

2. Explain why, outside the body, the risk of harm from alpha radiation is less than from beta or gamma radiation.

_____

_____ [2 marks]

3. Alexander Litvinenko was poisoned in 2006 by having radioactive polonium put in his tea which he then drank. Was the tea contaminated or irradiated? Explain your answer.

_____

_____ [2 marks]

Common misconception

If an object is **contaminated** radioactive material is left in the object. The radioactive material is not in contact with the object during **irradiation** – the radiation passes through, but no matter has been transferred.

4. Food is sometimes irradiated in order to kill harmful pathogens.
Explain why it is safe to eat irradiated food, unless the food comes into contact with the radioactive source.

_____

_____

_____

_____ [4 marks]

5. A person working at a nuclear power station must be protected from irradiation.

Describe **two** effects that irradiation can have on the cells in the human body.

_____

_____

_____ [2 marks]

Scalars and vectors

1. The diagram shows towns A and B, joined by a road. The distance measured in a straight line from town A to town B is 10 km. The distance along the road from A to B is 26 km.

Which statement correctly describes the displacement of town B from town A?
Tick **one** box.

26 km ☐   10 km due north ☐

10 km due east ☐   10 km ☐   [1 mark]

2. Which two quantities are scalar quantities? Tick **two** boxes.

Mass ☐   Displacement ☐   Time ☐   Force ☐   [2 marks]

3. Complete these sentences about vectors and scalars. Use answers from the box.

size	displacement	distance
direction	scalar	vector

A vector has both size and _____. A scalar has _____

but no direction. _____ is measured in a straight line from a start point to a

finish point. Distance is a _____ quantity.   [4 marks]

4. The diagram shows the path from X to Y, with three arrows representing displacement vectors.

What is the correct description of the three vectors that describe the path from X to Y?
Tick **one** box.

20 m east, 20 m north, 20 m east ☐

10 m west, 10 m north, 20 m west ☐

10 m east, 10 m north, 20 m east ☐

10 m east, 10 m north, 10 m east ☐   [1 mark]

Speed and velocity

1.

Maths

A car completes a journey of 100 km in 2.0 hours.

Calculate the average speed of the car in km/h.

Maths

You need to learn the equation that links distance travelled and average speed – it may **not** be given to you in a question. You also need to be able to rearrange equations.

Average speed = _____ km/h   [2 marks]

Worked Example

A student walks 1.1 km to school in a time of 15 minutes.

Calculate her average speed.

Rearranging $s = vt$ to make speed, v, the subject gives $v = \dfrac{s}{t}$

$$= \frac{1100 \text{ m}}{15 \times 60 \text{ s}}$$

$$= 1.2 \text{ m/s}$$

2.

Maths

An aircraft travels a distance of 50 km in a straight line due north in 250 s.

Calculate the aircraft's average velocity in m/s.

Remember

It is useful to know these typical speed estimates so you can check that your answers to velocity calculation questions are realistic: walking ≈ 1.5 m/s; jogging ≈ 3 m/s; cycling ≈ 6 m/s; car ≈ 20 m/s; aircraft ≈ 200 m/s.

Velocity = _____ m/s

Direction _____   [2 marks]

3.

Maths

What would be a suitable estimate for how long it takes an average runner to cover a distance of 1500 m?

Tick **one** box.

Maths

To round a number to three significant figures, look at the fourth digit. Round up if the digit is 5 or more, and round down if the digit is 4 or less.

For example, 1.620 67 rounds to 1.62.

5 s ☐   50 s ☐

500 s ☐   5000 s ☐   [1 mark]

4.

Maths

In athletics, the 100 m race is run on a straight track. A world-class sprinter wins the race in 9.90 s.

a At the finish line, what is his displacement?

Displacement = _____ m   [1 mark]

b What is his average velocity?

Give your answer to three significant figures.

Average velocity = _____ m/s   [3 marks]

5. The average speed of sound in air is 330 m/s.

Maths Calculate how much time it takes for the sound of a clap of thunder from a storm to be heard 1 km away.

Time = _____ s   [2 marks]

6. **a** A triathlete completes an iron man race which involves a swim, a cycle ride and a run. His times for the three stages of the race are shown in the table.

Maths

Complete the table to show his average speed for each of the three stages of the race.

> **Remember**
> To get the speed in m/s, you need to convert distances in km to m, and times in minutes to seconds.

Stage	Time (minutes)	Average speed (m/s)
1900 m swim	30	
90 km cycle	150	
21.1 km run	100	

[3 marks]

b Calculate the total distance he travels.

Total distance = _____ m   [1 mark]

c Calculate his average speed for the whole race.

Average speed = _____ m/s   [2 marks]

7. Here are different distance–time graphs for three different cars.

> **Remember**
> The gradient of an object's distance–time graph is equal to the speed of the object.

Describe the motion of each car. Use answers from the box.

getting faster	getting slower	not moving	steady speed

Car A: _____

Car B: _____

Car C: _____ [3 marks]

8.

Maths

Here is a distance–time graph for part of a car's journey on a test track.

a Determine the car's speed from the graph.

Speed = _____ m/s [2 marks]

> **Command word**
> When the question asks you to **determine**, you must use the data that is given to get your answer.

b What is the correct description of the car's motion? Tick **one** box.

Getting faster ☐ Steady speed ☐ Getting slower ☐ [1 mark]

9.

Maths

Here is a distance–time graph for a football falling vertically.

Use the graph to determine the speed of the football when it has a fallen a distance of 1.5 m.

Show clearly how you work out your answer.

Speed = _____ m/s [3 marks]

> **Remember**
> For the Higher Tier exam, you need to know that if an object's speed is changing, its speed at a certain time can be found by drawing a tangent and measuring the gradient of the tangent at that time.

> **Command words**
> The question asks you to show **how** you work out your answer from the graph. This means you **must** draw a line on the graph to show how you worked out your answer.

Acceleration

1. Calculate the acceleration of a car if its velocity increases from 2.0 m/s to 6.4 m/s in 4.0 s.

Maths

Acceleration = _____ m/s²   [2 marks]

Worked Example A lorry is travelling at a steady speed of 18 m/s. The driver then accelerates the lorry for 5.0 s until it reaches a speed of 23 m/s.
Calculate the lorry's acceleration.

$$acceleration = \frac{change\ in\ velocity}{time\ taken}$$

$$= \frac{23\ m/s - 18\ m/s}{5\ s} = 1.0\ m/s^2$$

Maths

You need to learn the equation for acceleration – it **may** not be given to you in a question.

2. A Formula 1 racing car can accelerate from a stationary position to 25 m/s in 2.1 s. Calculate the car's acceleration.

Maths

Give your answer to 2 significant figures.

Acceleration = _____ m/s²   [3 marks]

3. A cyclist is travelling along a straight road at a steady speed of 6.5 m/s. He pedals faster for 5.0 s and reaches a speed of 7.7 m/s.

Maths

Calculate his acceleration.

Give a unit with your answer.

Acceleration = _____ Unit _____   [3 marks]

4. This is a velocity–time graph for a car on a test track.

Maths

Describe the motion of the car between the times given. Use answers from the box.

constant velocity   stationary   deceleration   acceleration

0 to 5 seconds: _____

5 to 10 seconds: _____

10 to 15 seconds: _____

15 to 20 seconds: _____   [4 marks]

5.

Maths

The velocity-time graph for a sprinter during the first 2 seconds of a 100 m race is given below.

Calculate the sprinter's acceleration during the first 2 seconds of her race.

Remember

You need to know that the **gradient** of an object's velocity–time graph is equal to its **acceleration**.

Acceleration = _____ m/s²   [2 marks]

Worked Example

Use this velocity–time graph to calculate the sprinter's displacement during the first 2 s of the race.

Displacement = area of triangle formed by the line and the time axis up to the time of 2 s.

The area of a triangle is given by:

$$area = \frac{1}{2} \times base \times height$$

Displacement of the sprinter = $\frac{1}{2} \times 2$ s $\times 6$ m/s $= 6$ m

Remember

For the **Higher tier** exam you need to know that the **area** enclosed by the line and the time axis gives the object's **displacement**.

6.

Maths

This is the velocity–time graph for a car on a straight test track.

a For the first 3 s the car has uniform acceleration.

Calculate this uniform acceleration.

Acceleration = _____ m/s²   [2 marks]

b Between 6 and 8 s, the car has uniform deceleration.

Calculate this deceleration.

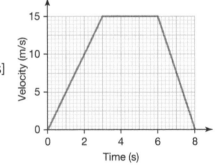

Deceleration = _____ m/s²   [2 marks]

Higher Tier only   **c** Calculate the car's displacement during the 8 s of its motion.

Displacement = _____ m   [2 marks]

7.

Maths

Higher
Tier only

This graph shows how the velocity of a sky diver changes from the moment she jumps out of the aircraft until her parachute opens.

Use the graph to estimate the distance she falls before opening her parachute.

Distance fallen = _____ m   [3 marks]

Equation for uniform acceleration

1.

Maths

A train, initially stationary at the platform, accelerates with an acceleration of 0.50 m/s².

Calculate the train's velocity when it has travelled a distance of 80 m.

Use the correct equation from the Physics Equation Sheet.

Maths

This equation is on the Physics Equation Sheet. You should be able to select and apply the equation – it may **not** be given in the question.

Train's velocity = _____ m/s   [2 marks]

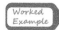

A sprinter accelerates from the start over the first 20 m with an acceleration of 2.5 m/s².

Calculate his velocity as he passes the 20 m mark.

First match the data to the equation symbols: $u = 0$, $a = 2.5$, $s = 20$.

Now substitute the data into the equation:

$v^2 - u^2 = 2as$

$v^2 - 0 = 2 \times 2.5 \times 20$

Which gives $v^2 = 100$ so his velocity at the 20 m mark is 10 m/s.

2.

Maths

A falling object on the Moon accelerates to the ground with an acceleration of 1.6 m/s². An astronaut on the Moon drops an object from a height of 1.3 m.

Calculate the object's velocity when it hits the ground.

Use the correct equation from the Physics Equation Sheet.

Object's velocity = _____ m/s   [2 marks]

3. An electric tram moving with a velocity of 5 m/s comes to a 50 m long straight section of track and accelerates with an acceleration of 0.30 m/s².

Maths

Calculate the tram's velocity when it has travelled the 50m along this straight section of track.

Use the correct equation from the Physics Equation Sheet.

Tram's velocity = _____ m/s   [2 marks]

Forces

1. Complete the sentences about forces. Use answers from the box.

friction	air resistance	gravitational
tension	normal contact	

Remember
'**Normal**' means at right angles. A normal contact force is a force at right angles to the surface where two objects are in contact.

The force in a rope being used in a tug-of-war is a _____ force.

The force exerted on the tyres of a bicycle when the cyclist is travelling along the road is a

_____ force.

The upward force exerted by the ground on a person standing is a

_____ force.

The _____ force is an example of a non-contact force.   [4 marks]

2. The diagram shows a box on the floor. The box is being dragged to the right by a person pulling the rope.

Add force vector arrows to represent the following forces. Label them, A, B, C and D, where force A (force of gravity) = 50 N; force B (normal contact force) = 50 N; force C (tension in the rope) = 25 N and force D (friction) = 25 N   [4 marks]

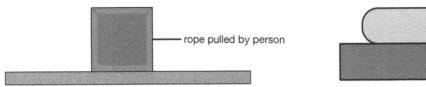

— rope pulled by person

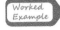

Worked Example The diagram shows a book on a table.

Draw arrows to represent the forces acting on the book.

Label the arrows with the names of the forces.

64

The two forces acting on the book in the diagram are the force of gravity exerted by the Earth and the normal contact force exerted by the table.

Since the book is not moving these two forces are the same size so their arrows must be drawn the same size.

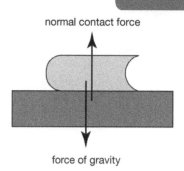

normal contact force

force of gravity

3. Identify the forces, *A*, *B*, *C*, *D*, *E*, *F* and *G* acting on the van in this diagram.

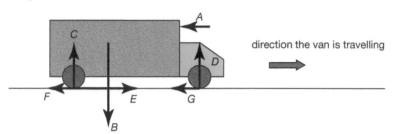

direction the van is travelling

A: _____   B: _____

C: _____   D: _____

E: _____   F: _____

G: _____   [7 marks]

Gravity and weight

1. Mass is the amount of substance in an object. Weight is the force of gravity on the object. Complete the sentences using answers from the box. Note that gravitational field strength at the Earth surface is greater than on the Moon.

increases	decreases	doesn't change

When an astronaut travels from the Earth to the Moon, his mass

_____ and his weight _____.   [2 marks]

2. *Curiosity*, NASA's Mars rover, has a mass of 900 kg.

Maths

Gravitational field strength at the Earth's surface = 9.8 N/kg

Gravitational field strength at the surface of Mars = 3.7 N/kg

Maths

The symbol for gravitational field strength is *g*. You need to know the equation for weight – it may not be given in a question.

a Calculate the weight of *Curiosity* on the Earth. Give the unit with your answer.

Weight on Earth = _____ Unit _____ [3 marks]

b Calculate the weight of *Curiosity* on Mars.

Weight on Mars = _____ Unit _____ [3 marks]

3. Weight and mass are described as being directly proportional. This relationship can be represented by the formula:

weight ∝ mass

Explain what is meant by describing weight and mass as being **directly proportional**.

_____

_____ [2 marks]

4. The diagram shows a block of wood.

Draw a cross on the diagram to mark the position of the centre of mass of the block.

Draw an arrow to represent the weight of the block. [2 marks]

5. **a** Name the apparatus used to measure the weight of an object.

_____ [1 mark]

b A student measures the weight of an object and obtains a value of 2.7 N. Calculate the mass of the object.

Gravitational field strength = 9.8 N/kg.

Mass of object = _____ N [2 marks]

6.

Maths

The fuel in a car's full tank of petrol has a mass of 4.3 kg. After a journey, the mass of fuel remaining in the tank is 2.6 kg.

Calculate the reduction in the car's weight as a result of the journey.

Give your answer to two significant figures.

Gravitational field strength = 9.8 N/kg.

Reduction in car's weight = _____ N   [4 marks]

Resultant forces and Newton's first law

1.

Maths

The diagram shows a child's trolley and the forces acting on it. One child exerts a force of 5 N in one direction and another child exerts a force of 11 N in the opposite direction.

Calculate the resultant force and state its direction.

Resultant force = _____ N

Direction _____   [2 marks]

2.

The diagram shows a crate being dragged along the ground by a person pulling a rope. The arrows show the pull on the rope and friction between the crate and the floor.

a   State Newton's first law as applied to a moving object.

_____

_____   [2 marks]

b   The crate is moving at a steady speed and the size of the pulling force is 50 N.

What is the resultant force on the crate?

Resultant force = _____ N   [1 mark]

3.

Higher Tier only

A sky diver with her parachute open is falling vertically at a steady speed towards the ground.

Draw a free body diagram in the box to represent the forces on the sky diver.

Label the diagram with the names of the forces acting on her.

[3 marks]

Remember
When drawing arrows to represent vectors, e.g. forces, the **length** of the arrow represents the **size** of the vector.

4.

Maths

Higher Tier only

The arrow in the diagram represents the tension force in the string in a kite that is flying.

20 N

a Complete the diagram to show the horizontal and vertical components of the tension force.

[2 marks]

b The arrow has been drawn to scale.

Determine the size of the vertical and horizontal components of the tension force.

Horizontal component = _____ N

Vertical component = _____ N   [2 marks]

Forces and acceleration

1.

Practical

The diagram shows a glider on an air track. Two light gates are placed above the track so that the card attached to the glider passes through the gates as the glider moves.

A student uses the apparatus to investigate acceleration and resultant force. The glider is accelerated by a weight that it is attached to it by string. The glider is released at the left end of the air track and passes through both light gates.

a What is the advantage of using the air track for motion experiments?

_____ [1 mark]

b What force on the glider is reduced by its streamlined shape?

_____ [1 mark]

c The card on top of the glider is 0.10 m wide. When the first weight is attached to the string the card passes through the light gate on the left in 0.77 s.

Use the equation

$$\text{speed} = \frac{\text{distance travelled}}{\text{time}}$$

to calculate the glider's velocity as it passes through the first gate.

Initial velocity of the glider = _____ m/s   [2 marks]

d The glider passes through the light gate on the right in a time of 0.30 s. Calculate the glider's velocity as it passes through the gate.

Give your answer to two significant figures.

Final velocity of the glider = _____ m/s   [3 marks]

e The distance between the light gates is 0.50 m.

Use the following equation to calculate the acceleration of the glider:

(final velocity)² − (initial velocity)² = 2 × acceleration × distance

> **Remember**
> This equation is on the Physics Equation Sheet. You should be able to select and apply the equation – it may **not** be given in the question.

Glider's acceleration = _____ m/s²   [2 marks]

f The student repeats the experiment with different weights attached to the string.

The student assumes that the force accelerating the glider is equal to the

> **Practical**
> **Anomalous** values, also known as **outliers**, are values which you judge not to be part of the variation due to random uncertainty.

weight attached to the string. The graph shows how she plots her results.

The student decides that one of the data sets is anomalous. She ignores the anomalous point and draws the line of best fit through the other points.

What should the student have done instead of ignoring the anomalous point?

_____

_____ [2 marks]

g What could the student conclude from the best fit line that she has drawn?

Explain your answer.

_____

_____ [2 marks]

2.

Maths

The engine driving force on a lorry is 4000 N. The total drag forces add up to 1200 N. The mass of the lorry is 2000 kg.

a Calculate the resultant force on the lorry.

Resultant force = _____ N   [1 mark]

b Use the equation $a = F \div m$ to calculate the lorry's acceleration.

Give the unit with your answer.

Lorry's acceleration = _____ Unit _____   [2 marks]

Worked Example

The engine driving force on a car is 2000 N. The total drag forces add up to 700 N. The mass of the car is 900 kg.

Calculate the car's acceleration.

The resultant force on the car = 2000 − 700 = 1300 N.

$F = ma$

so $a = F \div m$

= 1300 ÷ 900 = 1.4 m/s²

Maths

You need to learn the equation that links resultant force, mass and acceleration – it may **not** be given in the question.

70

3.

Maths

NASA's Falcon-9 rocket is launched to take a satellite into orbit. At launch the thrust from the rocket's engines is 8 200 000 N. The air resistance acting on the rocket is 600 000 N. The weight of the rocket is 5 500 000 N.

a State whether the thrust, the air resistance and the weight act upwards or downwards on the rocket.

Thrust: _____

Air resistance: _____

Weight: _____ [3 marks]

b Calculate the resultant force on the rocket during the launch.

Resultant force = _____ N [1 mark]

c Use the equation $a = F \div m$ to calculate the acceleration of the rocket given that its mass is 550 000 kg.

Acceleration = _____ m/s² [2 marks]

4.

Maths

a The diagram shows an apple falling from a tree. The forces on the apple as it falls are its weight and air resistance. The apple's weight is bigger than the air resistance.

motion of apple

Add arrows to the diagram to represent these two forces.

Label each arrow with the name of the force. [3 marks]

b The mass of the apple is 100 g. Give the apple's mass in kg.

Mass of apple = _____ kg [1 mark]

c Calculate the weight of the apple.

Gravitational field strength = 9.8 N/kg.

Weight of apple = _____ N [1 mark]

d If the air resistance is 0.30 N, calculate the resultant force on the apple.

Resultant force = _____ N   [1 mark].

e Calculate the acceleration of the apple.

Acceleration = _____ m/s²   [2 marks]

Terminal velocity

1. The diagram on the right shows a steel ball released at the surface of the oil in a glass tube. The ball reaches a terminal velocity at point C.

a At which position is the ball's acceleration at its maximum value?
Tick **one** box.

A ☐   B ☐   C ☐   [1 mark]

For parts **b**, **c** and **d**, choose your answers from this box.

not changing	increasing	zero	decreasing

b Describe the velocity of the sphere at positions A, B and C.

Position A: _____

Position B: _____

Position C: _____   [3 marks]

c Describe the acceleration of the sphere at positions B and C.

Position B: _____

Position C: _____   [2 marks]

d   Describe the resultant force of the sphere
    at positions B and C.

    Position B: _____

    Position C: _____

                                [2 marks]

Common misconception

Sometimes students make the mistake
of thinking that if the resultant force on a
moving object becomes zero, it will stop.
Newton's first law tells us that the object will
actually continue with a **constant velocity**.

2.   A skydiver jumps from an aircraft.

     After falling for 20 s she reaches her terminal velocity.

     During the fall, the vertical motion of the skydiver is affected by her weight and by air
     resistance.

     Describe how the skydiver's motion is affected by her weight and by air resistance during
     the first 20 s of her fall.

     _____

     _____

     _____

     _____

     _____

     _____   [4 marks]

Newton's third law

1.   When two objects interact they each exert a force on the other one.

     a   Which is the correct description of the directions of the two forces?
         Tick **one** box.

         Opposite direction ☐   Same direction ☐   [1 mark]

b Which is the correct description of the size of the two forces? Tick **one** box.

Same size ☐   Different size ☐   [1 mark]

c Which is the correct description of the type of forces acting? Tick **one** box.

Same type ☐   Different type ☐   [1 mark]

2. Complete the sentence to summarise Newton's third law by filling in the letters **A** or **B**.

If body A exerts a force on body B then body _____ exerts an equal but opposite force on

body _____.   [1 mark]

3. The diagram shows the forces acting on a box stationary on the floor.

force **B**

force **A**

a What type of force is force A?

_____ [1 mark]

b What type of force is force B?

_____ [1 mark]

Common misconceptions

The two forces in the diagram are equal in size and acting in opposite directions and some students may mistakenly think that these are a Newton's third law pair. They are **not**. The forces in a Newton's third law pair act on **different** objects.

c State the type, direction and the body acted upon by the force that forms the Newton's third law pair force with force A.

Type: _____

Direction: _____

Body acted upon: _____ [3 marks]

d State the type, direction and the body acted upon by the force that forms the Newton's third law pair force with force B.

Type: _____

Direction: _____

Body acted upon: _____ [3 marks]

4. In a rocket engine, exhaust gases at high pressure and temperature are produced by combustion of the rocket fuel with an oxidiser in the combustion chamber.

Use Newton's third law to explain how this results in the rocket being propelled upwards.

_____

_____

_____ [2 marks]

Work done and energy transfer

1. A person is pushing a shopping trolley at a steady speed at a supermarket.

> **Maths**
> You need to learn the equation for work done – it may **not** be given in the question.

Maths **a** They push the trolley a distance of 10 m with a horizontal force of 15 N.

Calculate the work done by the force in moving the trolley 10 m.

Give a unit with your answer.

Work done = _____ Unit _____ [3 marks]

b Since the trolley is being pushed at a steady speed, the resultant force on the trolley must be zero.

Name the other horizontal force that must be acting on the trolley.

State its direction.

Name of force: _____

Direction of force: _____ [2 marks]

c Describe how the different energy stores change as the shopper is pushing the trolley.

_____

_____ [2 marks]

2.

Maths

The diagram shows a winch dragging a 200 kg load up a slope in a loading bay. The winch exerts a force of 1000 N.

Remember
The definition of work depends on the force used and the distance moved in the direction of the force. Look carefully at the diagram to see what direction the force moves, and so which distance measurement to use.

a Use the equation $W = Fd$ to calculate how much work is done by the winch in dragging the container the 15 m up the slope.

Work done = _____ J   [2 marks]

b Use the equation $E_p = mgh$ to calculate the gravitational potential energy store gained by the load when it is 6.5 m above the floor.

Gravitational field strength = 9.8 N/kg.

Gain in gravitational potential energy store = _____ J   [2 marks]

c The work done by the winch is greater than the gravitational potential energy store gained by the load. Give **one** reason for this.

_____   [1 mark]

3.

Maths

a A small aircraft flies at a constant altitude at constant velocity of 100 m/s. The thrust from the engine is 800 N.

Calculate the useful work done by the engine when the aircraft travels 100 m.

Remember
Power is equal to the work done per second.

Useful work done by the engine = _____ J   [2 marks]

b What is the useful output power of the aircraft's engine?

Useful output power of the engine = _____ W   [1 mark]

Stopping distance

1. A car is being driven at 15 m/s (about 34 mph). The mass of the car including the driver is 800 kg.

Maths

a Write down the equation which links speed, kinetic energy and mass.

_____ [1 mark]

Calculate the kinetic energy store of the car.

Kinetic energy store of the car = _____ J   [2 marks]

b The driver sees a hazard in the road ahead. He needs to stop his car before the hazard is reached. During the time it takes time for the driver to react to the situation the car carries on moving at 15 m/s. The driver is alert and his reaction time is 0.60 s.

Use the equation

distance travelled = speed × time

to calculate the distance travelled by the car while the driver is thinking about the situation.

Thinking distance = _____ m   [2 marks]

c The driver applies the brakes creating a braking force of 5000 N. For the car to stop, all its kinetic energy has to be dissipated when work is done by the brakes.

Use the equation

work done = force × distance

to calculate the distance over which the braking force must act to stop the car.

Braking distance = _____ m   [2 marks]

d Calculate the car's total stopping distance.

Stopping distance = _____ m   [1 mark]

2.

A car is being driven at 30 m/s (about 68 mph). The mass of the car including the driver is 800 kg.

a Calculate the kinetic energy store of the car.

Kinetic energy store of the car = _____ J   [2 marks]

b Calculate the thinking distance in this situation, if the driver's reaction time is 0.60 s.

Thinking distance = _____ m   [2 marks]

c The car's braking system creates a braking force of 5000 N.

Calculate the distance over which the braking force must act to stop the car.

Braking distance = _____ m   [2 marks]

d Calculate the car's stopping distance.

Stopping distance = _____ m   [1 mark]

e Compare the stopping distance for a car travelling at 15 m/s with a car travelling at 30 m/s (use your answers to **1d** and **2d**).

Complete the sentence:

If the speed of a car is doubled then the distance that a car travels before it can stop

is _____ times bigger.   [1 mark]

3. Give **two** factors which could increase a driver's reaction time.

_____

_____   [2 marks]

4.

Maths

Three of the factors which can affect a car's overall stopping distance include an icy road, car speed and driver tiredness.

stopping distance = braking distance + thinking distance

For each factor, describe and explain how a car's **thinking distance** or **braking distance** is affected if the car is required to stop in an emergency.

_____

_____

_____

_____

_____

_____

_____ [6 marks]

5. **a** Describe what happens to the car's store of kinetic energy when a car driver applies the brakes, bringing the car to a stop.

_____

_____ [1 mark]

b How are the car's brakes affected by the car's braking?

_____ [1 mark]

c A car is travelling at 30 mph (13 m/s). The driver does an emergency stop. Her car stops in a shorter distance than that predicted by the graph.

Suggest how the brakes might be affected by this rapid deceleration.

What effect could this have on the car?

Command words

This question asks you to **make suggestions**. Your answer should **link** what you already know and the information in the question.

_____

_____ [2 marks]

d When a car rapidly decelerates during an emergency stop, the driver's body also decelerates rapidly.

What exerts the force on the driver to cause her to decelerate?

_____ [1 mark]

Force and extension

1. The diagram shows a spring before and after it has been stretched.

Maths

a Stretching or compressing a spring needs two forces to act on the spring.

Which **two** objects in the diagram are exerting forces on the spring to make it stretch?

1 _____ 2 _____ [2 marks]

b Calculate the extension of the spring in metres.

> **Remember**
> You need to know that the extension of a spring is found by **subtracting** its unstretched length from its stretched length

Extension = _____ m   [1 mark]

c Use the equation below to calculate the elastic potential energy E_e, stored in the stretched spring. The spring constant is 35 N/m.

Give your answer to two significant figures.

$$E_e = \frac{1}{2} \times \text{spring constant} \times (\text{extension})^2$$

Elastic potential energy = _____ J   [3 marks]

2.

A student is given four springs. Each one has a different value for its spring constant, k. So some of the springs are easy to stretch and some are harder to stretch. She adds weights to each spring to produce a stretching force, F, and measures the extension, e.

The table below shows her results.

Maths

You need to learn the equation that links the force applied to a spring to its extension – it may **not** be given to you in a question.

a Use the equation force = spring constant × extension to complete the last column in the table.

Spring number	Force F (N)	Extension e (m)	Spring constant k (N/m)
1	5.0	0.25	
2	3.0	0.10	
3	2.0	0.20	
4	4.0	0.10	

[4 marks]

b Which spring is the easiest to stretch?

Spring number _____ [1 mark]

c Which is the stiffest spring?

Spring number _____ [1 mark]

3.

Practical

If vertical distance measurements are to be made with a clamped metre rule, first check that the rule is vertical. You can do this with a plumb line.

A student is given the apparatus shown in the diagram to investigate the relationship between extension and stretching force for a spring.

The weight attached to the spring causes a stretching force on the spring.

The metre rule is positioned so that a pointer taped to the spring points to a value on the metre rule that gives the spring's length.

The student's measurements are shown in the table on the next page.

a The unstretched length of the spring is 5.0 cm.

Complete the last column of the student's table of measurements to show the extension values of the spring in cm.

Stretching force (N)	Length of spring (cm)	Extension (cm)
0.50	7.3	
1.00	9.5	
1.50	11.8	
2.00	14.1	
2.50	16.4	
3.00	18.7	

[2 marks]

b Suggest why a heavy weight has been placed on the base of the stand.

_____ [1 mark]

c The student plots the measurements in the table on a graph of extension versus stretching force.

The student concludes that extension ∝ stretching force.

State what this means.

_____

_____ [1 marks]

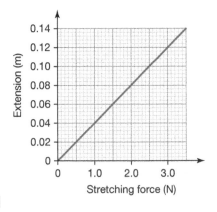

d Explain how the graph supports this conclusion.

_____

_____ [2 marks]

e The student is given a stone and asked to find its weight using the apparatus and the graph above. He attaches the stone to the spring. The stone causes an extension of 11.0 cm.

Use the graph to determine the weight of the stone. Show on the graph how you obtained the answer.

Weight = _____ N   [2 marks]

Momentum

1.

Use the equation $p = mv$ to work out the units for momentum.

Higher Tier only

Units of momentum _____ [1 mark]

Maths

You need to learn the equation for momentum – it may **not** be given in the question.

2.

a Is momentum a vector or scalar quantity? Tick **one** box.

Higher Tier only

Vector ☐ Scalar ☐ [1 mark]

b Explain your answer to part **a**.

_____ [2 marks]

3.

A car of mass 800 kg is travelling due west on a straight section of road at a speed of 20 m/s.

Maths

Calculate the car's momentum.

Higher Tier only

Give the unit with your answer.

Momentum = _____ due west

Unit _____ [3 marks]

4.

A 0.057 kg tennis ball is travelling at 100 km/hr.

Maths

Calculate the size of the ball's momentum.

Higher Tier only

Give your answer to 2 significant figures.

Momentum = _____ kg m/s [4 marks]

5.

The motion of an 800 kg car on a straight test track is shown in the graph.

Maths

Use the diagram to calculate the size of the car's momentum at 1 s, 2 s and 3 s after the start of the car's motion.

Higher Tier only

Show clearly how you work out your answer.

Momentum at 1 s: _____ kg m/s

Momentum at 2 s: _____ kg m/s

Momentum at 3 s: _____ kg m/s   [3 marks]

6. A car of mass 800 kg has momentum equal to 1200 kg m/s.

What is the velocity of the car?

Car's velocity = _____ m/s   [2 marks]

Conservation of momentum

1. State what is meant by 'conservation of momentum'.

_____

_____   [1 mark]

2. Two rugby players are running and collide head-on with each other. The collision stops both players in their tracks and they drop to the ground. An instant after the collision their total momentum is zero so their total momentum before the collision must also be zero.

Explain how this could be possible.

_____

_____

_____   [2 marks]

Transverse and longitudinal waves

1. Which **one** of the following statements is true? Tick **one** box.

Waves transfer matter but no energy. ☐

Waves transfer energy but no matter. ☐

Waves do not transfer either energy or matter. ☐ [1 mark]

2. Complete the sentences. Use words from the box.

perpendicular parallel

In transverse waves the oscillations are _____ to the direction of motion of

the wave. In longitudinal waves the oscillations are _____ to the direction

of motion of the wave. [2 marks]

3. **a** Give **one** example of a transverse wave.

_____ [1 mark]

b Give **one** example of a longitudinal wave.

_____ [1 mark]

4. Look at the diagram of a spring below.

a State whether the diagram shows a longitudinal or transverse wave.

_____ [1 mark]

b Label on the diagram an example of a compression. [1 mark]

c Label on the diagram an example of a rarefaction. [1 mark]

5. A toy boat floats on a pond. A boy throws a stone in the water and a ripple travels across the water surface.

   a State the direction in which the toy boat moves as the wave passes.

   _____ [1 mark]

   b Explain why the wave does not make the boat move closer to the edge of the pond.

   _____

   _____ [2 marks]

Frequency and period

1. The diagram shows the displacement of a water wave.

   On the diagram, label:

   a The amplitude   [1 mark]

   b The wavelength   [1 mark]

2. a Define the frequency of a wave. Give its unit.

   _____

   Unit: _____   [2 marks]

   b Define the wavelength of a wave. Give its unit.

   _____

   Unit: _____   [2 marks]

   c Define the period of a wave. Give its unit.

   _____

   Unit: _____   [2 marks]

3. The equation below gives the relationship between the time period, T and frequency, f of a wave.

Maths

$$T = \frac{1}{f}$$

Maths

This equation is on the Physics Equation Sheet. You should be able to select and apply the equation – it may **not** be given in the question.

a Calculate the time period of a wave with a frequency of 10 Hz.

Time period = _____ s   [2 marks]

b Calculate the frequency of a wave with a time period of 0.5 s.

Frequency = _____ Hz   [3 marks]

c Calculate the time period of a wave with a frequency of 5 kHz.

Maths

Whenever you substitute a value in an equation, check that the value has standard units. If not, **convert** the value before substituting into the equation. Remember that a 'k' in front of a unit means 'kilo', so 5 kHz means 5000 Hz.

Time period = _____ s   [2 marks]

Wave speed

1. Which one of the following does wave speed depend on? Tick **one** box.

Medium (the material wave is travelling through) ☐

Amplitude ☐   [1 mark]

2. **a** Write down the formula which links wave speed, frequency and wavelength.

Maths

You need to learn this equation – it may **not** be given to you in a question.

_____   [1 mark]

State the units of measurement for the following quantities:

Wave speed _____

Frequency _____

Wavelength _____   [3 marks]

3.   Look at the graph of a water wave below.

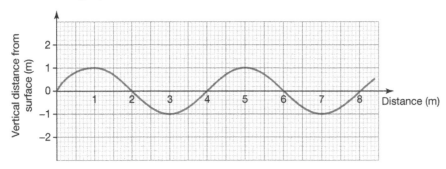

a   Use the graph to determine:

The amplitude of the wave

_____

The wavelength of the wave

_____   [2 marks]

> **Command word**
>
> When the question asks you to **determine**, you must use the data that is given to get your answer. Do **not** measure with a ruler unless the question tells you to measure.

b   The wave is travelling at 5 m/s.

Calculate the frequency of the wave.

Use the correct equation from the Physics Equation Sheet.

Frequency = _____ Hz   [3 marks]

4.   10 water waves pass a point every minute.

Maths

a   Calculate the frequency of these waves.

Frequency = _____ Hz   [2 marks]

b The wavelength is 2 m.

Calculate the speed of the wave.

Wave speed = _____ m/s   [2 marks]

5. A source produces 100 waves every 10 minutes.

Calculate the frequency of these waves in Hz. Give your answer to two significant figures.

Frequency = _____ Hz   [3 marks]

6. Describe a method for determining the speed of sound in air.

Practical Include in your description:

- the measurements and calculations you would make
- why the results will not be very accurate and how you could improve the accuracy.

_____

Practical

You should write the method in steps that follow on from each other and could be followed by someone else. You can do this by writing **first, next, then**. Or, you could use numbered points or subheadings.

_____

_____

_____

_____

_____

_____   [6 marks]

7. A student produces waves in a ripple tank.

Practical **a** Describe how the student could measure the frequency of the waves.

_____

_____   [2 marks]

b Another student is trying to measure the wavelength of the water waves with a ruler held over the waves.

Give **one** reason it is difficult to measure wavelength this way.

Suggest an improvement.

_____

_____ [2 marks]

c One way of working out the speed of the waves as they travel through the water is to measure the wave speed and frequency and use the equation:

> wave speed = frequency × wavelength

Describe how the student could work out the speed of the waves **without** using a wavelength measurement.

Maths

Think of another equation for speed which might help here – in fact it is the equation which **defines** the quantity of speed.

_____

_____

_____ [2 marks]

Refraction of waves

. . . .

1. Complete the ray diagram to show the path of the ray of light as it passes through and leaves a glass block. [3 marks]

Common misconception

You may think that the ray coming out of the block should be in a different direction to the ray entering the block. However, if the block has **parallel** sides, the change in angle as the ray enters the block is reversed when the ray leaves the block. The ray is offset, but **parallel** to the path of the original ray.

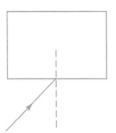

2.

a Complete the ray diagram in the diagram to show how the wave fronts change when they enter the glass block and when they leave again.

Remember

You can think of wave fronts as adjacent peaks of a wave – these points on the wave are moving up and down **together** at the same time and are one wavelength apart.

[3 marks]

b As a light ray passes into water from air, it changes direction.

State why the direction of the wave changes at the boundary between air and water.

_____ [1 mark]

The electromagnetic spectrum

1. Complete the sentences. Use words from the box.

longitudinal	transverse	frequencies
speeds	highest	lowest

Electromagnetic waves are _____ waves. Electromagnetic waves

have a spectrum of different _____ . Gamma rays have the

_____ frequencies. Radio waves have the _____

wavelength. [4 marks]

2. Complete the sentence.

The whole of the electromagnetic spectrum has the same _____. [1 mark]

3. **a** Name **one** part of the electromagnetic spectrum with a smaller wavelength

than ultraviolet. _____ [1 mark]

b Name **one** part of the electromagnetic spectrum with a lower frequency than

microwaves. _____ [1 mark]

c State which has the longer wavelength: red or violet light.

_____ [1 mark]

4. The equation that links the wave speed, wavelength and
frequency of a wave is

wave speed = frequency × wavelength

Use this equation to explain why parts of the electromagnetic
spectrum with large wavelengths also have low frequencies.

Maths
You need to learn the wave
equation – it may **not** be
given to you in a question.

_____

_____ [2 marks]

5. An electromagnetic wave has speed 3×10^8 m/s and wavelength 1×10^{-8} m.

Calculate its frequency.

Use the correct equation from the Physics Equation Sheet.

_____ [3 marks]

Investigating infrared radiation

1.

Practical

The diagram shows a large metal cube. One side is painted with a matt white paint, another with a matt black paint and another with a shiny black paint. The other sides are left unpainted.

The can is filled with very hot water. An infrared detector is clamped at the same distance from each side. After five minutes the readings are noted.

The table shows the results.

a Which surface radiates energy most quickly per square metre? Tick **one** box.

Bare metal ☐

Matt black ☐

Matt white ☐

Shiny black ☐

Surface	Reading (W/m²)
bare metal	2
matt black	10
matt white	8
shiny black	8

[1 mark]

b Name a piece of apparatus that could be used, instead of the infrared detector, to compare the amount of infrared radiation emitted from each surface.

_____ [1 mark]

c Suggest **one** advantage of the infrared detector compared to the piece of apparatus you have named.

_____ [1 mark]

2. Infrared radiation is a type of electromagnetic wave.

Which statement about infrared radiation is **incorrect**? Tick **one** box.

Black and white T-shirts absorb different amounts of infrared radiated from the Sun. ☐

Infrared radiation has a shorter wavelength than visible light. ☐

Thermal energy can be transferred by infrared radiation. ☐

Uses and hazards of the electromagnetic spectrum

1. Draw **one** line to match each part of the electromagnetic spectrum with an example given of its use.

Electromagnetic wave	Use
Radio waves	Electric heaters, cooking food, night-vision cameras
Microwaves	Television and radio
Infrared	Energy efficient lamps, sun tanning
Visible light	Medical imaging and treatments
Ultraviolet	Satellite communications, cooking food
X-rays and gamma rays	Fibre optic communications

[6 marks]

2. State why X-rays can be used for medical imaging.

_____ [1 mark]

3. Name the type of electromagnetic radiation that can cause skin cancer and premature skin aging.

_____ [1 mark]

4. Name the type of electromagnetic radiation used in remote controls.

_____ [1 mark]

5. State the **three** parts of the electromagnetic spectrum that can be most harmful to humans.

State the reason why they can harm living tissue.

_____

_____

_____ [2 marks]

6. The Sun emits radiation at all wavelengths in the electromagnetic spectrum.

Higher Tier only

Only visible light, some infrared, some ultraviolet, microwaves and radio waves are transmitted through the Earth's atmosphere.

a Which property of electromagnetic waves does the transmission depend on?

_____ [1 mark]

b State what happens to the gamma and X-rays.

_____ [1 mark]

7. Radio waves and microwaves are both used to broadcast television and radio signals. Satellites are sometimes used to transmit television programmes. These television signals are sent to, and received from, the satellites using microwaves.

Higher Tier only

a State why microwaves can be used for satellite communications, but radio waves cannot.

_____ [1 mark]

b Firefighters use infrared cameras to help locate people in smoke-filled buildings.

Explain why it is possible to locate a person using infrared radiation, when you cannot see them using visible light.

_____

_____ [2 marks]

8. The recommended radiation dose limit every 5 years for people who work with radiation is 0.1 Sv.

Synoptic

A spine X-ray exposes each person in the room to a dose of 1.5 mSv.

Maths

a Calculate the recommended dose limit every 5 years in mSv.

Maths

Remember that 'm' in front of a unit means 'milli', so there are **1000** mSv in 1 Sv.

Recommended 5-year dose limit = _____ mSv [1 mark]

b State whether a patient should be worried about having an X-ray on their spine due to the radiation dose.

Give a reason for your answer.

_____

_____ [1 mark]

c A radiographer doing multiple spine X-rays a day is worried about the radiation dose.

Show that they are right to be concerned.

_____

_____ [3 marks]

d Describe how the risk to the radiographer could be reduced.

_____ [1 mark]

---

9. Which two statements about gamma rays are correct? Tick **two** boxes.

Gamma rays are emitted from the electrons in an atom. ☐

Gamma rays are not harmful to human body tissue. ☐

Gamma rays are emitted from the nucleus of an atom. ☐

Gamma rays are ionising radiation. ☐

10.

Higher Tier only

A source of gamma rays in the form of a tracer can be used for obtaining images inside the human body to help diagnose diseases.

Explain what properties of gamma rays make them suitable for this application.

_____

_____

_____ [2 marks]

Radio waves

1. State **two** uses of radio waves.

1 _____

2 _____ [2 marks]

2. Complete the sentences about the properties of radio waves.

Radio waves have _____ energy and _____ frequency

compared to the rest of the electromagnetic spectrum. They have a _____
wavelength than microwaves. [3 marks]

3. Describe how a radio transmitter produces radio waves.

Higher Tier only

_____

_____ [2 marks]

4. Describe how radio waves affect a radio receiver.

Higher Tier only

_____

_____ [2 marks]

5. State the quantity which is the same in the alternating current in a radio receiver
as it is in the radio wave itself.

Higher Tier only

_____

_____ [1 mark]

Magnets and magnetic forces

. . . .

1. Complete the sentences. Use words from the box.

attract	repel

When two permanent magnets are close to each other, like poles of the magnets

_____ and unlike poles _____.   [2 marks]

2. Which two of the following materials are magnetic?

Tick **two** boxes.

Aluminium ☐   Nickel ☐   Cobalt ☐   Copper ☐   [2 marks]

3. A magnet is brought close to another magnet.

Describe where the force between the two magnets is largest.

_____   [1 mark]

4. State whether magnetism is a contact or non-contact force.

Explain your answer.

_____

_____   [2 marks]

5. Describe the difference between a permanent magnet and an induced magnet.

_____

_____

_____

_____   [4 marks]

Analysing the question

Look at the number of marks available. It is not likely that you will be able to fit everything into a single sentence. Talk in detail about **both** types of magnet, one at a time.

Magnetic fields

1. Describe what is meant by a magnetic field.

_____ [1 mark]

2. Which two of the following would be attracted to the north pole of a magnet?

Tick **two** boxes.

Steel ☐

Lead ☐

The north pole of another magnet ☐

The south pole of another magnet ☐ [2 marks]

3. If you wished to pick up a steel car with a magnet, which part of the magnet would you place near to the car?

Explain your answer.

Remember
Field lines are closest together at the poles of a magnet – think about how it might apply to this question.

_____

_____ [2 marks]

4. Magnetic field lines point in the direction of the force that would act on another north pole placed in the field at that point.

Use this information to state whether field lines point towards the **north** or **south** pole of a permanent magnet.

_____ [1 mark]

5. A magnetic compass points towards geographic north. However, when the compass is brought near a permanent magnet, its direction changes.

Suggest **two** differences between the field of the permanent magnet and the Earth's magnetic field.

_____

_____ [2 marks]

6. Describe how to plot the magnetic field pattern of a magnet using a plotting compass.

_____

_____

_____ [3 marks]

The magnetic effect of a current

1. Describe an experiment to demonstrate that a wire carrying a current generates a magnetic field. You have access to a plotting compass, a battery, and a long wire.

_____

_____

_____ [3 marks]

2. **a** The line in the diagram 1 below represents a wire that is carrying a current.

On diagram 2, sketch the shape and direction of the magnetic field around the wire.

Command words

Although 'sketch' means you only need to show the **approximate** shape, you should still take care with the drawing. You will **not** gain the mark if the field lines cross or if the arrows show contradictory directions.

card

card

Diagram 1   Diagram 2

[2 marks]

b State **two** ways you could increase the strength of the field without any more equipment.

_____

_____ [2 marks]

c The direction of the current is reversed.

State what happens to the direction of the lines in the magnetic field pattern.

_____ [1 mark]

3. A solenoid is shown in the diagram.

S pole   N pole

a The wire is wrapped around a material that makes the magnetic field of the solenoid stronger.

Name this material.

_____ [1 mark]

b Draw on the diagram the pattern of magnetic field lines inside and outside the solenoid. [3 marks]

4. Describe how to construct an electromagnet.

You may wish to use a diagram as part of your answer.

_____

_____

_____ [3 marks]

5. Look at the diagram.

Describe how to use a compass to plot the shape and direction of the magnetic field produced by the wire when a current passes through the wire.

card

_____

_____

_____

_____ [4 marks]

Fleming's left-hand rule

1. A conductor carrying a current is placed between the poles of two magnets, at right angles to the magnetic field.

Higher Tier only

a State what happens.

_____ [1 mark]

b Explain why this occurs.

_____

_____ [2 marks]

c State the name of the effect that this experiment demonstrates.

_____ [1 mark]

2. Look at the diagram.

Higher Tier only

a On the diagram, draw an arrow to show which way the wire will move when the switch is closed.

battery

S

N

switch

[1 mark]

b Describe **two** ways in which the force on the wire could be increased.

_____

_____ [2 marks]

Common misconception

Remember that in Fleming's left-hand rule the direction of the current represented by your middle finger is conventional current, which flows from positive to negative.

Worked Example

The current in a conductor is 2 A. The conductor has length of 0.1 m and is placed in a magnetic field with flux density 0.25 T.

Calculate the force on the conductor.

Use

force = magnetic flux density × current × length

Force = 0.25 × 2 × 0.1

= 0.05 N

Maths

This equation is on the Physics Equation Sheet. You should be able to select and apply the equation – it may **not** be given in the question.

3.

Higher Tier only

The current in a conductor is 3 mA and it is placed in a magnetic field with flux density 0.5 T and has a length of 2 m. The wire is at 90° to the direction of the magnetic field.

Calculate the force on the conductor.

Maths

Remember that the values you substitute in the equation must be in metres (for length) and amps (for current). 1 mA is 0.001 A.

Force = _____ N [2 marks]

4.

Higher Tier only

A current-carrying conductor at right angles to a magnetic field experiences a force of 0.5 N. The conductor has a length of 10 cm and a current of 0.1 A.

Calculate the magnetic flux density of the permanent field it is in.

Magnetic flux density = _____ T [2 marks]

Electric motors

1. The diagram shows an electric motor. The arrows on the sides of the coil show the direction of the conventional current.

a Label the direction of the magnetic field on the diagram.

[1 mark]

b Use Fleming's left-hand rule to label the direction of the force on the left-hand side of the coil.

[1 mark]

c Use Fleming's left-hand rule to label the direction of the force on the right-hand side of the coil.

[1 mark]

d State the direction of motion of the coil.

_____ [1 mark]

e After half a turn, the coil is horizontal again.

State what needs to happen to ensure the motion continues in the same direction.

_____ [1 mark]

f Explain how this is achieved. Refer to the diagram to help you.

_____

_____ [2 marks]

g Describe **three** ways in which you could make the motor spin faster.

_____

_____

_____ [3 marks]

Section 1: Energy changes in a system

Energy stores and systems

1. Walking along a flat road [1 mark]
2. [1 mark for each correct line. If more than one line is drawn from a system, no marks for that system.]

4. Elastic potential, kinetic, kinetic, thermal [1 mark each]

Calculating energy changes

1. a $E_k = \frac{1}{2}mv^2$ or

   kinetic energy = 0.5 × mass × speed^2

   b $\frac{1}{2} \times 900 \times (4)^2$ [1 mark] = 7200 J [1 mark]
2. a GPE = $m \times g \times h$ [1 mark]

   b $2.0 \times 9.8 \times 2.0$ [1 mark] = 39.2 (J) [1 mark]
3. a $50 \times 9.8 \times 5.0$ [1 mark] = 2450 [1 mark] unit: J [1 mark]

   b 2350 J [1 mark]
4. a $\frac{1}{2} \times 800 \times 10^2$ [1 mark] = 40 000 (J) [1 mark]

   b $\frac{1}{2} \times 800 \times 5^2$ [1 mark] = 10 000 (J) [1 mark]

   c 40 000 J − 10 000 J = 30 000 J [1 mark]

   d Energy transferred as thermal energy [1 mark] to the brakes / surroundings. [1 mark]
5. $\frac{1}{2} \times 20 \times (0.1)^2$ [1 mark] = 0.1 (J) [1 mark]
6. a 0.12 m (or 12 cm) [1 mark]

   b $\frac{1}{2} \times 25 \times 0.12^2$ [1 mark] = 0.18 J [1 mark]
7. a At point of release: elastic potential energy to kinetic energy. [1 mark] Stone travelling upwards towards its maximum height: kinetic energy to gravitational potential energy. [1 mark] Stone falling back towards ground: gravitational potential energy to kinetic energy. [1 mark]

   b $1.0 = 0.05 \times 9.8 \times h$ [1 mark] so height = 1.0/(0.05 × 9.8) [1 mark] = 2.04(08) [1 mark] = 2.0 (to 2 sig figs) [1 mark]

Calculating energy changes when a system is heated

1. $0.5 \times 4200 \times 80$ [1 mark] = 168 000 J (or 168 kJ) [1 mark]
2. a 23 °C [1 mark]

   b $c = \frac{\Delta E}{m\Delta\theta}$ [1 mark] $= \frac{21260}{1 \times 23}$ [1 mark] = 924 [1 mark]

   c Reduce store of thermal energy transferred to surroundings [1 mark]

   d Some thermal energy store transferred to surroundings / used to raise temperature of immersion heater [1 mark]
3. a Gravitational potential, kinetic, gravitational potential [1 mark each]

   b $250 \times 9.8 \times 60$ [1 mark] = 147 000 J [1 mark]

   c $250 \times 790 \times 0.5$ [1 mark] = 98 750 J [1 mark] 99 000 J [1 mark]
4. a $1.0 \times 4200 \times 80$ [1 mark] = 336 000 J [1 mark]

   b $0.5 \times 500 \times 80$ [1 mark] = 20 000 J [1 mark]

   c Total energy supplied = 336 000 + 20 000 = 356 000 J [1 mark]

Work and power

1.

The force of gravity pulling a free-wheeling cyclist faster and faster down a hill	From chemical energy store to kinetic energy store
A person pushing a heavy shopping trolley to get it moving	From chemical energy store to gravitational potential energy store
A person lifting a box from the floor onto a shelf	From gravitational potential energy store to kinetic energy store

2. a 10×15 [1 mark] = 150 J [1 mark]

   b 150/10 [1 mark] = 15 W [1 mark]

3. a 4000×50 [1 mark] = 200 000 J [1 mark]

   b 200/5 [1 mark] = 40 kW [1 mark] (or 200 000/5 and kW conversion)

4. a $mgh = 800 \times 9.8 \times 10$ [1 mark] = 78 400 J [1 mark]

   b $\dfrac{78\,400}{20}$ [1 mark] = 3920 W [1 mark]

Conservation of energy

1. Dissipation [1 mark]

2. Energy can be destroyed [1 mark]

3. 165 J [1 mark]

4. Decreases (to zero), force of friction (between ground and rotating wheels), same / constant / conserved, thermal energy store of wheels and surroundings [1 mark each]

Ways of reducing unwanted energy transfers

1. Lubricate wheels [1 mark]

2. Decrease the thermal conductivity of the walls [1 mark] Increase the thickness of the walls [1 mark]

3. a polyurethane [1 mark]

   b Increasing the thickness of the insulation in the loft of a house <u>decreases</u> the rate of energy transfer by conduction through the insulation. [1 mark]

When the heating system in a house is switched off, the house cools down. Increasing the thickness of the loft insulation <u>decreases</u> the rate of cooling of the house. [1 mark]

Efficiency

1. a chemical, kinetic, thermal [1 mark each]

   b 580 MJ [1 mark]

   c 0.42 [1 mark] 42% [1 mark]

2. 0.8 = useful output energy/500 MJ [1 mark] useful output energy = 0.8×500 MJ [1 mark] = 400 MJ [1 mark]

3. 0.5 = 1000 MJ/useful input energy transfer [1 mark] useful input energy transfer = 1000 MJ/0.5 [1 mark] = 2000 MJ [1 mark]

4. Any **two** of: loft insulation, cavity wall insulation, preventing draughts, double glazing [1 mark each]

National and global energy resources

1. a Coal and gas [1 mark for both]

   b Uranium [1 mark]

   c Energy resource is finite / will eventually run out [1 mark] because not replenished [1 mark]

   d Any **three** from [1 mark each]:
- Biggest changes between 2013 and 2015 involve coal and renewables.
- Percentage of electricity generated by coal decreased by 15%.
- Percentage of electricity generated by renewables increased by over 10%.
- Only small changes / no trend for gas and nuclear.

   e Any **three** from [1 mark each]:
- Burning coal causes emission of carbon dioxide / contributes to climate change.
- Use of nuclear fuel does **not** result in carbon dioxide emission / does **not** cause climate change.
- Burning coal produces soot particles / pollution / acid rain from sulfur dioxide.
- Use of nuclear fuel produces radioactive waste.
- Radioactive waste will be a hazard for hundreds of years.

2. a Any **one** of: wood chips, wood waste, agricultural waste, waste from sugar cane processing [1 mark]

b So electricity always available / to avoid power cuts [1 mark]

c Both unreliable sources. Wind: no wind = no electricity, [1 mark] solar: no electricity when dark [1 mark]

3. Marks in three bands according to level of response.

Level 3 [5–6 marks]: Clear coherent description of trends in energy consumption over time for industry, transport and homes involving several comparisons. Logical possible explanation for why trends occurred.
Level 2 [3–4 marks]: Some valid comparisons made of trends in energy consumption over time. Some valid suggestions made, with reasons. There may be some incorrect or irrelevant points.
Level 1 [1–2 marks]: Major trends in energy consumption for industry, transport and homes identified but no direct comparisons. Suggested explanations are vague with few correct and relevant points.
Level 0 [0 marks]: No relevant content.

Points that should be made:

- Largest increase between 1970 and 2014 is in energy consumed by transport.
- Increase in population means more vehicles on the road, more vehicles from Europe since joining EU, more people driving.
- Largest decrease between 1970 and 2014 is in energy consumed by industry.
- Industry more efficient in its use of energy, less heavy industry in UK in 2014 than in 1970.
- Small increase in the energy consumed by homes between 1970 and 2014.
- Increasing population (and household income) means more energy consumed.
- In recent years there has been a reduction in consumption by transport and homes.
- Appliances used in homes and vehicles are more efficient.

4. Any **two** from [1 mark each]:

- UK heating systems / appliances / vehicles / industry now more efficient.
- Many other countries becoming more industrialised.

- Industry in developing countries may not use energy efficiently.
- Large increase in number of cars / vehicles used around the world.

Circuit diagrams

1.

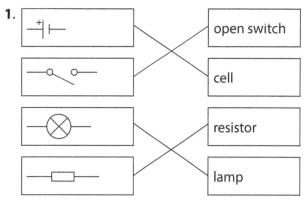

2. Four [1 mark]

3. a X [1 mark] **b** Z [1 mark]
  c Y [1 mark] **d** W [1 mark]

Electrical charge and current

1. Same, [1 mark] current same at any point in a circuit made up of a single (closed) loop. [1 mark]

2. a Charge [1 mark]

  b Cell [1 mark]

  c [2 marks for voltmeter connected across lamp]

  d 0.15×20 [1 mark] $= 3.0$, [1 mark] coulomb or C [1 mark]

  e $\dfrac{1}{20 \times 10^{-3}}$ [1 mark] 50 (s) [1 mark]

Electrical resistance

1.

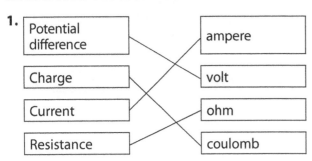

Potential difference → volt

Charge → coulomb

Current → ampere

Resistance → ohm

2. [1 mark each for cell, ammeter and voltmeter correctly positioned]

3. a 0.25×6 [1 mark] $1.5\ \Omega$ [1 mark]

b Ammeter reading / current would decrease [1 mark]

c $\dfrac{1.5}{48 \times 10^{-3}}$ [1 mark] $= 31.25\ \Omega$ [1 mark] $31\ \Omega$ [1 mark]

4. a 4.47, 5.60, 6.71, 7.84, 8.98, 9.93 [2 marks for 6 answers correct] 3 significant figures [1 mark]

b Same thickness / diameter of wire / same temperature [1 mark]

c Spot anomalies, [1 mark] reduce effect of random errors [1 mark]

d *x*-axis: length (of wire), [1 mark] *y*-axis: resistance [1 mark]

e Open switch between measurements [1 mark]

Resistors and I–V characteristics

1. a Variable resistor [1 mark]

b [1 mark for variable resistor symbol connected between X and Y]

c Reverse battery connections [1 mark]

d Current is directly proportional to p.d., [1 mark] graph = straight line, [1 mark] passing through origin [1 mark]

2. a Resistance, [1 mark] temperature [1 mark]

b Non-linear [1 mark]

c Large [1 mark]

3. Marks in three bands according to level of response.

Level 3 [5–6 marks]: Detailed and coherent plan with all major steps described in correct logical sequence. Plan addresses issues of obtaining repeatable measurements and negative values of current and p.d.
Level 2 [3–4 marks]: Detailed and coherent plan with all major steps described in correct logical sequence. Some detail may be missing.
Level 1 [1–2 marks]: Simple steps related to relevant apparatus, steps may not be given in correct logical sequence.
Level 0 [0 marks]: No relevant content.

Points that should be made:
• Current through X measured using ammeter. • p.d. across X measured using voltmeter. • Repeatedly adjust variable resistor to change current through X or change p.d. (across X). • Connections to the battery are reversed. • Obtain a range of negative current and p.d. readings.
• Repeat procedure to obtain repeat readings of current for each p.d. value. • Average repeat current values. • Plot line graph of current against p.d. • If line of best fit can be drawn that closely matches all data points, this indicates a proportional relationship.

4. a p.d. [1 mark]

b $\dfrac{1.51}{3.52 \times 10^{-3}}$ [1 mark] $= 492$ [1 mark]

c $\dfrac{1.51}{1.23 \times 10^{-3}}$ [1 mark] $= 1230$ [1 mark]

d Resistance lower [1 mark] as LDR receives increasing amounts of light [1 mark] (accept converse description) [allow resistance changes depending on the amount of light that hits the LDR for 1 mark]

5. a Thermistor symbol shown connected between X and Y [1 mark]

b Resistance decreases as thermistor's temperature increases [2 marks] [Allow only 1 mark for temperature of the thermistor changes as its resistance changes.]

Series and parallel circuits

1. a Resistors in series, [1 mark] same current through all three resistors. [1 mark]

b 6.6 Ω [1 mark]

c 0.5 V [1 mark]

2. a All three resistors have same p.d. across them, [1 mark] resistors in parallel [1 mark]

b $\frac{1.5}{5}$ [1 mark] = 0.3 A [1 mark]

3. a $\frac{1.5}{15}$ [1 mark] = 0.1 A [1 mark]

b $\frac{1.5}{10}$ [1 mark] = 0.15 A [1 mark]

Mains electricity

1. a 50 Hz [1 mark]

b 230 V [1 mark]

2.

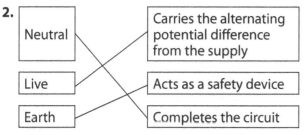

3. alternating, brown, earth [1 mark each]

4. Any **three** of: if the fault occurs, there is a p.d. between metal casing and ground / earth, [1 mark] if person touches casing, current could pass through person, [1 mark] earth wire carries current to ground instead,

[1 mark] because of very low resistance, [1 mark] protecting person from electric shock / preventing current passing through person. [1 mark]

Energy changes in circuits

1. Kinetic, thermal [1 mark each]

2. Operate vacuum cleaner for longer period of time, [1 mark] use vacuum cleaner with higher power rating [1 mark]

3. 2000 × 30 × 60 [1 mark] = 3 600 000 J [1 mark]

4. a 1000 × 5 × 60 [1 mark] = 300 000 J [1 mark]

b $\frac{300\,000}{230}$ [1 mark] = 1304 C [1 mark]

5. a 2 × 10 × 60 [1 mark] = 1200 J [1 mark]

b $\frac{1200}{3}$ [1 mark] = 400 C [1 mark]

Electrical power

1. 230 × 2.0 [1 mark] = 460 [1 mark] W [1 mark]

2. $P = I^2R$ [1 mark] = 4.0^2 × 0.4 [1 mark] = 6.4 W [1 mark]

3. Microwave A lower power (600 W), [1 mark] microwave B higher power (900 W), [1 mark] so microwave B transfers energy more quickly / at higher rate. [1 mark]

4. a 230 × 0.40 [1 mark] = 92 W [1 mark]

b 92 × 10 × 60 [1 mark] = 55 200 J [1 mark]

The National Grid

1. When all power stations are connected, the National Grid can supply electricity to any town / city. If each town / city depended on its own power station then if there was a problem with the power station the town / city would have a power cut. [1 mark]

2. Increases, decreases, [2 marks] decreases, increases [2 marks]

3. Transformer A is a step-up and transformer B is a step-down [1 mark]

4. The National Grid transmits electricity at high voltages to improve efficiency. [1 mark] The National Grid transmits electricity at low currents to improve efficiency. [1 mark]

5. Kettle cable [1 mark]

Section 3: Particle model of matter

Density

1. Density $= \dfrac{mass}{volume}$ or $\rho = \dfrac{m}{V}$ [1 mark]

2. $740 = 3.7/mass$ [1 mark] mass $= 3.7/740$ [1 mark] $= 0.005$ [1 mark] m^3 [1 mark]

3. a Micrometer [1 mark]

 b Measuring cylinder [1 mark]

4. a Marks in three bands according to level of response.

Level 3 [5–6 marks]: Method described in detail including equation required to calculate density. Steps in an order that makes sense and could be followed by someone else to obtain valid results. Some valid suggestions about reducing errors are made, with reasons.
Level 2 [3–4 marks]: Method described clearly but some detail may be missing and steps may not be in an order that makes sense. At least one valid suggestion about reducing errors made, with reasons.
Level 1 [1–2 marks]: Basic description of measurements needed with no indication of how to use them or reduce errors.
Level 0 [0 marks]: No relevant content.
Points that should be made:
• Measure mass using a balance.
• Calculate density using $\rho = m/V$.
• Fill displacement can with water until full up to spout.
• Submerge rock in water.
• Measure volume / mass of water displaced (with a measuring cylinder).
• Volume of water displaced = volume of rock.
• Do repeats and calculate mean.
• Reference to avoiding systematic errors (e.g. reading measuring cylinder at eye level or taking account of meniscus or ensuring balance is zeroed).

 b Marks in two bands according to the level of response.

Level 2 [3–4 marks]: Evidence set out clearly to reach a conclusion. Correct density calculated for sample and correct conclusion drawn.
Level 1 [1–2 marks]: Correct use of equation and attempt to compare to one of the given densities. Response may not be structured coherently.
Level 0 [0 marks]: No relevant content.
Points that should be made:
• Calculate density using $\rho = m/V$
• Correct value 3600 kg/m^3 (2 sig figs).
• Data show that sample is more likely to be a meteorite as it is closer to this density range.
• Outside expected density range for terrestrial rock.

5. Marks in two bands according to level of response.

Level 2 [3–4 marks]: Method described in detail including equation required to calculate density. Steps in an order that makes sense and could be followed by someone else to obtain valid results.
Level 1 [1–2 marks]: Basic description of measurements needed with no indication of how to use them.
Level 0 [0 marks]: No relevant content.
Points that should be made:
• Need to work out mass and volume as density = mass/volume.
• Put an empty measuring cylinder on some scales and note its mass.
• Add some of liquid and note new mass.
• Take away new mass from mass of empty measuring cylinder to work out mass of liquid.
• Divide mass of liquid by volume in measuring cylinder.

 a Very few circles / do not occupy more than about one third of box, [1 mark] no circles touching [1 mark]

 b A gas bubble displaces a volume of liquid equal to its own volume, [1 mark] weight of gas bubble much less than weight of same volume of water (because less dense), [1 mark] causing resultant force (upthrust) on gas bubble. [1 mark]

Changes of state

1. a

Freeze	gas to liquid
Boil	solid to liquid
Condense	liquid to gas
Melt	liquid to solid

b Boil, [1 mark] melt [1 mark]

2. Changes state from solid to gas with no liquid phase. [1 mark]

3. The change is reversible / material has its original properties if change is reversed. [1 mark]

4. Burning [1 mark]

5. Student B, [1 mark] because no particles lost / gained [1 mark]

Specific heat capacity and latent heat

1. In hot gas: faster / higher speed / more k.e. [1 mark]

2. Kinetic energy [1 mark]

3. a Particles moving more quickly on average. [1 mark]

b Bath has far more particles / greater mass [1 mark] so total energy of particles greater. [1 mark]

4. Despite having same temperature so same kinetic energy, [1 mark] water particles have greater internal energy because energy was supplied / gained for change of state to occur. [1 mark]

5. Energy is used to change state of material [1 mark] instead of increasing kinetic energy store of particles. [1 mark]

6. a

b Melting

c $5 \times 45\,000$ [1 mark] = $225\,000$ [1 mark]

7. $15\,000 = 0.5 \times L$ [1 mark] $L = 15\,000/0.5$ [1 mark] = $30\,000$ J/kg [1 mark]

Particle motion in gases

1. Due to force of collisions with walls of container. [1 mark]

2. They move more / faster / with more kinetic energy. [1 mark]

3. Pressure will increase [1 mark] because more frequent collisions, [1 mark] more force in collisions [1 mark]

4. a Bung will pop out or flask will shatter. [1 mark]

b As temperature increases, particles move around more quickly [1 mark] resulting in increased pressure. [1 mark]

5. Marks in two bands according to the level of response.

Level 2 [3–4 marks]: Detailed explanation with logical links between clearly identified relevant points.
Level 1 [1–2 marks]: Relevant, but separate, points are made. Logic may be unclear.
Level 0 [0 marks]: No relevant content.

Points that should be made:

- Hot jam heats the layer of air above.
- Layer of hot air trapped by lid / no air can escape.
- Initially high gas pressure.
- Heated air cools over time.
- This lowers gas pressure (same volume).
- This means there is greater pressure on top of lid (from atmospheric pressure) than underneath.
- This makes jar difficult to open / so more force needed.

6. The molecule could collide with another molecule. [1 mark]

The molecule could collide with the walls of the container. [1 mark]

Protons, neutrons and electrons

1. [1 mark for each correct entry]

proton	positive	1	inside
neutron	neutral	1	inside
electron	negative	negligible	outside nucleus

2. nucleus, further, lower [1 mark each]

3. Absorbed some radiation [1 mark] so electrons are further from nucleus / occupy a higher energy level [1 mark]

The size of atoms

1. $10^{-5}, 10^1, 10^3, 10^4$ first and last correct, [1–2 marks] all correct [all 4 marks]

2. 2×10^{-3} m [1 mark]

3. A football pitch [1 mark]

4. a A [1 mark]

   b C [1 mark]

Elements and isotopes

1. neutral, electrons, protons, atomic, protons / neutrons, neutrons / protons [1 mark each]

2. [1 mark for each correct entry]

Atomic number	Mass number	Number of protons	Number of neutrons
6	12	6	6
11	13	11	12
27	59	27	32
13	27	13	14

3. Atoms of same element, [1 mark] with same number of protons / same atomic number [1 mark] but different numbers of neutrons / different mass number [1 mark]

4. a 27, 33, 27 [1 mark each]

   b $^{60}_{27}$Co [1 mark]

   c $^{59}_{27}$Co [1 mark]

Electrons and ions

1.

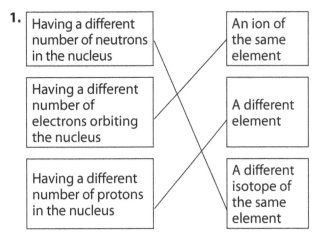

Having a different number of neutrons in the nucleus	An ion of the same element
Having a different number of electrons orbiting the nucleus	A different element
Having a different number of protons in the nucleus	A different isotope of the same element

2. Positively charged [1 mark] because atoms neutral / equal numbers of positive and negative charge [1 mark] so losing electron (negatively charged) means more protons than electrons. [1 mark]

3. 17, 18, 18 [1 mark each]

4. 13, 14, 11 [1 mark each]

Discovering the structure of the atom

1. Discovery of electron [1 mark]

2. a Ball / sphere of positive charge [1 mark] with negative electrons embedded throughout. [1 mark]

   b Concentrated in a small space [1 mark]

3. Instead of electrons surrounding the nucleus anywhere in a cloud, [1 mark] Bohr described electrons as only able to occupy certain energy levels / distances from nucleus. [1 mark]

4. Protons [1 mark] and neutrons. [1 mark]

5. a Grey box = alpha source [1 mark] gold square = thin gold foil [1 mark]

   b All the alpha particles would go straight through. [1 mark]

   c Most alpha particles went straight through [1 mark] (some were deflected / scattered at small angles) and very few (approx. 1 in 8000) bounced back / were scattered (deflected) back to the source. [1 mark]

6. Marks in three bands according to level of response.

Level 3 [5–6 marks]: Clear and detailed explanation. Experiment results clearly and logically tied to correct conclusions / features of model.
Level 2 [3–4 marks]: An attempt to link conclusions / features of model to results but logic used may not be clear.
Level 1 [1–2 marks]: Explanations vague and not linked to results.
Level 0 [0 marks]: No relevant content.

Points that should be made:

- Small central nucleus where most of mass is concentrated.
- Nucleus is charged.
- Electrons surround nucleus.
- Most alpha particles went straight through, implying atom is mostly empty space.
- Most alpha particles do not go near enough to the nucleus to be deflected.
- Some are deflected implying the positively charged alpha particles are repelled by a positively charged 'nucleus'.
- Very few bounced back, implying there is a very small, dense positive area we now call the nucleus.

Radioactive decay

1. (Nuclear) electron [1 mark]
2. nucleus, unstable, random, becquerels / Bq, count rate [1 mark each]
3. **a** Neutron [1 mark]
   b Beta [1 mark]
   c Gamma (ray) [1 mark]
   d 2 protons, [1 mark] 2 neutrons. [1 mark] (only 1 mark for 'helium nucleus')
   e A neutron decays into a proton and an electron. [1 mark] The electron is emitted from the nucleus. [1 mark]

Comparing alpha, beta and gamma radiation

1. [1 mark for each correct entry]

beta	**thin sheet of aluminium**	**a few metres (accept 1–3 m)**
gamma	several cm of lead	**very far**
alpha	**paper**	1–2 cm

2. **a** Causes atoms to become ions [1 mark]
   b Alpha [1 mark]
3. Beta will not penetrate body so radiation emitted by tracer cannot be detected outside body / beta very ionising so dangerous to use as tracer. [1 mark]
4. **a** Beta because it penetrates through outer layer of skin / alpha does not. [1 mark]
   b Best to limit penetration depth [1 mark] so fewer side effects to other organs and body tissues. [1 mark]
5. Gamma would pass straight through so count rate measured on other side of paper would not change with thickness. [1 mark] Alpha absorbed by paper and air between emitter and detector, whatever the thickness of the paper. [1 mark] Beta absorbed more by thick paper than thin paper, so gives different readings for different thicknesses. [1 mark]

Radioactive decay equations

1. $^{4}_{2}$He [1 mark]
2. $^{0}_{-1}$e [1 mark]
3. $^{14}_{6}$C $\rightarrow$ $^{14}_{7}$N + $^{0}_{-1}$e, 1 mark for 7, 1 mark for $^{0}_{-1}$e
4. 225 [1 mark] $^{4}_{2}$He [1 mark]
5. 209 [1 mark] 83 [1 mark]
6. **a** Beta / (nuclear) electron [1 mark]
   b $^{60}_{28}$ [1 mark] $^{0}_{-1}$e [1 mark]

Half-lives

1. The average time it takes for the activity of the sample to halve. [1 mark]
2. **a** Attempt to read off graph from count rate 400 to 200 (or other pair of values) [1 mark] 30 +/− 2 s [1 mark]
   b 6 times for count rate to halve [1 mark] 6 × answer to part a = 180 s [1 mark]
3. Record background count-rate, [1 mark] deduct this from each measurement. [1 mark]
4. **a** [2 marks for points plotted correctly] (1 mark for one plotting error, 0 if more)
   b Smooth curve, not dot-to-dot straight lines [1 mark]
   c 3.8 +/− 0.2 [1 mark]
   d 3.8 +/− 0.2 [1 mark]
   e 5 half-lives to get to 6 counts/s [1 mark] working: 5 × their answer to **c**) [1 mark] 19 +/− 1 [1 mark]

5. 3 half-lives [1 mark] so 3 × 6 hours [1 mark] = 18 hours [1 mark]

6. 3 half-lives [1 mark] = 600 years in total / 3 [1 mark] = 200 years [1 mark]

Radioactive contamination

1. a Any **two** of: thin sheet of aluminium or equivalent between you and source, increase distance to source, reduce exposure time [1 mark each]

  b Any **two** of: sheet of lead between you and source, increase distance to source, reduce exposure time [1 mark each]

2. Hard to be irradiated by alpha as it is absorbed by 1 or 2 cm air [1 mark] and by clothes or dead skin cells. [1 mark]

3. Contaminated, [1 mark] because contamination involves contact with radioactive source, not just having radiation emitted pass through. [1 mark]

4. Marks in two bands according to level of response.

Level 2 [3–4 marks]: Detailed explanation with logical links between clearly identified relevant points.
Level 1 [1–2 marks]: Relevant, but separate, points are made. Logic may be unclear.
Level 0: No relevant content.
Points that should be made:
• Food is safe to eat when irradiated as no radioactive material has been in contact with the food.   • Radiation does not make the food radioactive.   • So no radiation emitted by food when it is inside body.   • If food comes into contact with radioactive source it is contaminated.   • Contamination harmful as when food was ingested it would emit radiation inside body.   • This is ionising, so can harm cells.

5. Any **two** of the following [1 mark each]:

The cell may die.

The nucleus of the cell may be damaged.

The cell may become cancerous.

Scalars and vectors

1. 10 km due east [1 mark]

2. Mass, [1 mark] time [1 mark]

3. Direction, size, displacement, scalar [1 mark each]

4. 10 m east, 10 m north, 20 m east [1 mark]

Speed and velocity

1. $\frac{100}{2.0}$ [1 mark] = 50 km/h [1 mark]

2. Velocity = 200 m/s [1 mark] direction: north [1 mark]

3. 500 s [1 mark]

4. a 100 m [1 mark]

  b 100/9.9 [1 mark] = 10.1 m/s [1 mark] 3 sig figs [1 mark]

5. Time taken = 3 s [2 marks]

6. a 1.1, [1 mark] 10, [1 mark] 3.5 [1 mark]

  b 113 000 m [1 mark]

  c 113 000/(280 × 60) [1 mark] = 6.7 m/s [1 mark]

7. A: steady speed, B: not moving, C: getting slower [1 mark each]

8. a Gradient = $\frac{150}{10}$ [1 mark] = 15 m/s [1 mark]

  b Steady speed [1 mark]

9. Tangent drawn to the gradient at distance 1.5 m, [1 mark] substitution of values in $\frac{\text{change in } Y}{\text{change in } X}$, [1 mark] estimate in range of 4–6 m/s [1 mark]

Acceleration

1. $\frac{6.4 - 2.0}{4.0}$ [1 mark] = 1.1 m/s² [1 mark]

2. $\frac{25}{2.1}$ [1 mark] = 11.9(0476) [1 mark] = 12 (to 2 sig figs) [1 mark]

3. $\frac{7.7 - 6.5}{5}$ [1 mark] = 0.24 [1 mark] m/s² [1 mark]

4. 0–5 seconds: constant velocity, [1 mark] 5–10 seconds: acceleration, [1 mark] 10–15 seconds: constant velocity, [1 mark] 15–20 seconds: deceleration [1 mark]

5. $\frac{\text{change in } Y}{\text{change in } X} = \frac{6}{2}$ [1 mark] = 3 m/s² [1 mark]

6. a $\frac{15}{3}$ [1 mark] = 5 m/s² [1 mark]

 b $\frac{15}{2}$ [1 mark] = 7.5 m/s² [1 mark]

 c $\left(\frac{1}{2} \times 3 \times 15\right) + \left(3 \times 15\right) + \left(\frac{1}{2} \times 2 \times 15\right)$

 [1 mark] = 82.5 m [1 mark]

 (1 mark for marking correct area on graph)

7. Number of squares in enclosed area = 34 [1 mark] area of each square = 5 × 10 = 50 m [1 mark] distance = 1700 m [1 mark]

Equation for uniform acceleration

1. $v^2 - 0 = 2 \times 0.5 \times 80$ [1 mark] $v = \sqrt{80} = 8.9$ m/s [1 mark]

2. $v^2 - 0 = 2 \times 1.6 \times 1.3 = 4.16$ m/s, [1 mark] $v = \sqrt{4.16} = 2.0$ m/s [1 mark]

3. $v^2 - 25 = 2 \times 0.3 \times 50$ [1 mark] $v = \sqrt{55} = 7.4$ m/s [1 mark]

Forces

1. tension, friction, normal contact, gravitational [1 mark each]

2. One mark for each correct arrow. [4 marks] Note: arrows for C and D should be the same length. Arrows for A and B should be the same length but twice the length of C and D.

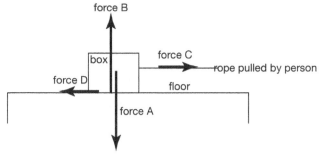

3. A = air resistance, B = gravitational force, C = normal contact force, D = normal contact force, E = engine driving force, F = friction, G = friction [1 mark each]

Gravity and weight

1. Doesn't change [1 mark] decreases [1 mark]

2. a 900 × 9.8 [1 mark] = 8820 [1 mark] N [1 mark]

 b 900 × 3.7 [1 mark] = 3330 [1 mark] N [1 mark]

3. Multiplying mass by a constant factor, such as 2 [1 mark] causes weight to also be multiplied by 2 [1 mark]

4. X at centre, [1 mark] arrow downwards from X [1 mark]

5. a Newtonmeter [1 mark]

 b 2.7 ÷ 9.8 [1 mark] = 0.28 N [1 mark]

6. Reduction in mass = 1.7 kg, [1 mark] reduction in weight = 1.7 × 9.8 [1 mark] = 16.66 [1 mark] = 17 (to 2 sig figs) [1 mark]

Resultant forces and Newton's 1st law

1. 6 N [1 mark] direction: left [1 mark]

2. a If resultant force on moving object is zero [1 mark] object continues to move at same speed and in same direction. [1 mark]

 b 0 N [1 mark]

3. [1 mark each for correctly labelled forces] [1 mark for arrows same length]

air resistance (drag)

weight

4. a [1 mark each for correct length and position of a component]

 b Horizontal = 14 N, [1 mark] vertical = 14 N [1 mark]

Forces and acceleration

1. a Air track removes friction [1 mark]

 b Air resistance / drag [1 mark]

 c $\frac{0.10}{0.77}$ [1 mark] = 0.13 m/s [1 mark]

 d $\frac{0.10}{0.30}$ [1 mark] = 0.33(3) [1 mark] = 0.33 (2 sig figs) [1 mark]

e $(0.33)^2 - (0.13)^2 = 2 \times$ acceleration $\times 0.5$ [1 mark] acceleration = 0.092 m/s² [1 mark]

f Repeat the anomalous measurement. [1 mark] If same result is obtained, either repeat all measurements [1 mark] or include anomalous point when drawing the best fit line. [1 mark]

g Acceleration is directly proportional to force. [1 mark] Best fit line is straight and passes through origin. [1 mark]

2. a 2800 N [1 mark]

b 1.4 [1 mark] m/s² [1 mark]

3. a Thrust: upwards, air resistance: downwards, weight: downwards [1 mark each]

b 2 100 000 N [1 mark]

c 2 100 000 ÷ 550 000 [1 mark] = 3.8 m/s² [1 mark]

4. a [1 mark for each correctly labelled arrow] [1 mark if weight arrow longer than air resistance arrow]

air resistance
motion of apple
weight

b 0.10 kg [1 mark]

c 0.98 N [1 mark]

d 0.68 N [1 mark]

e $a = \dfrac{0.68}{0.1} = $ [1 mark] = 6.8 m/s² [1 mark]

Terminal velocity

1 a A [1 mark]

b A: increasing, B: increasing, C: not changing [1 mark each]

c B: decreasing, C: zero [1 mark each]

d B: decreasing, C: zero [1 mark each]

2. Marks in two bands according to the level of response.

Level 2 [3–4 marks]: Changes to the relative sizes of weight and air resistance and the resulting effect on the skydiver's speed described coherently and in the correct sequence.
Level 1 [1–2 marks]: Some relevant content regarding weight or air resistance.
Level 0 [0 marks]: No relevant content.

Points that should be made:

- Initially the weight is bigger than the air resistance.
- (Initially) the skydiver accelerates downwards.
- As the speed increases, the air resistance increases.
- When the air resistance becomes equal to the weight, the resultant force becomes zero.

Newton's third law

1. a Opposite direction [1 mark]

b Same size [1 mark]

c Same type [1 mark]

2. B, A [1 mark]

3. a Gravitational force [1 mark]

b Normal contact force [1 mark]

c gravitational, upwards, the Earth [1 mark each]

d normal contact, downwards, the floor / Earth [1 mark each]

4. Combustion chamber exerts downward force on exhaust gases, [1 mark] exhaust gases exert upward force on combustion chamber of the rocket. [1 mark]

Work done and energy transfer

1. a 15×10 [1 mark] = 150 [1 mark] J (accept N m) [1 mark]

b Friction, [1 mark] opposite to direction trolley is moving [1 mark]

c Chemical energy store in shopper's body decreases, [1 mark] thermal energy store of surroundings increases. [1 mark]

2. a 1000×15 [1 mark] = 15 000 J [1 mark]

b $200 \times 9.8 \times 6.5$ [1 mark] = 12 740 = 13 000 J [1 mark]

c Some energy is dissipated as thermal energy. [1 mark]

3. a 800×100 [1 mark] = 80 000 J [1 mark]

b 80 000 W [1 mark]

Stopping distance

1. **a** Kinetic energy = $\frac{1}{2}mv^2$ [1 mark] $0.5 \times 800 \times 15^2$ [1 mark] = 90 000 J [1 mark]

   b 15×0.60 [1 mark] = 9.0 m (accept 9) [1 mark]

   c $5000 \times d = 90\,000$ [1 mark] $d = 18$ m [1 mark] (allow error carried forward)

   d 27 m [1 mark] (allow error carried forward)

2. **a** $0.5 \times 800 \times 30^2$ [1 mark] = 360 000 J [1 mark]

   b 30×0.60 [1 mark] = 18 m [1 mark]

   c $5000 \times d = 360\,000$ [1 mark] $d = 72$ m [1 mark]

   d 90 m [1 mark]

   e If speed of a car is doubled then distance that car travels before it can stop is 3.3 times bigger. [1 mark]

3. Any **two** from: tiredness, distracted by something, has drunk alcohol, has taken drugs [1 mark each]

4. Marks in three bands according to the level of response.

Level 3 [5–6 marks]: Coherent description and explanation for all three factors using appropriate scientific terminology.
Level 2 [3–4 marks]: Clear description and explanation for at least two factors.
Level 1 [1–2 marks]: Some relevant content describing the effects of at least two factors but may lack suitable explanation.
Level 0 [0 marks]: No relevant content.

   Points that should be made:

   - An icy road reduces the braking force.
   - So an icy road increases the braking distance.
   - More (kinetic) energy must be removed to stop a car travelling at a higher speed.
   - So braking distance increases at higher speeds.
   - A tired driver has a longer reaction time.
   - So if the driver is tired the thinking distance is increased.

5. **a** Transferred to thermal energy store in brakes. [1 mark]

   b Temperature increases [1 mark]

   c Brake temperature rises more rapidly [1 mark] which may cause them to overheat and be less effective. [1 mark]

   d Seat belt [1 mark]

Force and extension

1. **a** clamp, [1 mark] weight [1 mark]

   b 0.05 m [1 mark]

   c $\frac{1}{2} \times 35 \times 0.05^2$ [1 mark] = 0.044 J [1 mark] 2 sig figs [1 mark]

2. **a** 20, 30, 10, 40 [1 mark each]

   b 3 [1 mark]

   c 4 [1 mark]

3. **a** 2.3, 4.5, 6.8, 9.1, 11.4, 13.7 [2 marks]

   b To prevent the stand from toppling over. [1 mark]

   c Extension is directly proportional to stretching force. [1 mark]

   d Graph is a straight line [1 mark] through the origin. [1 mark]

   e Weight in range 2.7–2.8 N, [1 mark] one line drawn on graph from 0.11 m to best fit line and second line vertically downwards to stretching force axis. [1 mark]

Momentum

1. kg × m/s = kg m/s [1 mark]

2. **a** Vector [1 mark]

   b Momentum = mass × velocity, [1 mark] velocity is a vector [1 mark]

3. 800×20 [1 mark] = 16 000 [1 mark] kg m/s [1 mark]

4. Convert 100 km/h to 27.8 m/s [1 mark] 0.057×27.8 [1 mark] = 1.6 kg m/s [1 mark] 2 sig figs [1 mark]

5. 4800 kg m/s, 6400 kg m/s, 4000 kg m/s [1 mark each]

6. $1200 \div 800$ [1 mark] 1.5 m/s [1 mark]

Conservation of momentum

1. Total momentum before event is equal to total momentum after event, **or** (total) momentum stays the same. [1 mark]

2. Because the rugby players are running in opposite directions, one has positive momentum and the other has negative momentum. [1 mark] If their value for mass times velocity is the same then their momentum can add up to zero. [1 mark]

Transverse and longitudinal waves

1. Waves transfer energy but no matter. [1 mark]

2. perpendicular, [1 mark] parallel [1 mark]

3. **a** Water waves / electromagnetic waves [1 mark]

   b Sound waves [1 mark]

4. **a** Longitudinal [1 mark]

   b Correctly labelled where coils most bunched [1 mark]

   c Correctly labelled where coils furthest apart [1 mark]

5. **a** Vertically, up and down [1 mark] (Allow particles at surface move in a circle **if** also state that there is no overall horizontal movement.)

   b Wave moves water (and boat) up and down only, [1 mark] wave travels outwards (from source) but no water travels outwards [1 mark]

Frequency and period

1. amplitude

wavelength

   a [1 mark if amplitude labelled correctly]

   b [1 mark if wavelength labelled correctly]

2. **a** Number of complete waves produced / passing a point each second. [1 mark] hertz / Hz [1 mark]

   b Distance between two points on a wave and equivalent point on the adjacent wave moving in phase. [1 mark] metres / m [1 mark]

   c Time for one complete wave to pass a point [1 mark] (allow reciprocal or inverse of frequency), seconds / s [1 mark]

3. **a** 1/10 [1 mark] = 0.1 s [1 mark]

   b Rearrange formula [1 mark] 1/0.5 [1 mark] = 2 Hz [1 mark]

   c 1/5000 [1 mark] = 0.0002 s [1 mark]

Wave speed

1. Medium [1 mark]

2. **a** wave speed = frequency × wavelength [1 mark]

   b m/s / metres per second, [1 mark] Hz / hertz, [1 mark] m / metres [1 mark]

3. **a** 1 m, [1 mark] 4 m [1 mark]

   b Rearrangement [1 mark] 5/4 [1 mark] = 1.25 Hz [1 mark]

4. **a** 10/60 per second [1 mark] = 0.167 Hz [1 mark]

   b 0.167 × 2 [1 mark] = 0.334 m/s [1 mark]

5. 100/600 [1 mark] = 0.166(6) [1 mark] = 0.17 Hz (2 sig figs) [1 mark]

6. Marks in three bands according to level of response.

Level 3 [5–6 marks]: Method described in detail including equation required to calculate speed. Steps in an order that makes sense and could be followed by someone else to obtain valid results. Some valid suggestions about reducing errors made, with reasons.
Level 2 [3–4 marks]: Method described clearly but some detail may be missing and steps may not be in an order that makes sense. At least one valid suggestion about reducing errors made, with reasons.
Level 1 [1–2 marks]: Basic description of measurements needed with no indication of how to use them or reduce errors.
Level 0: No relevant content.
Points that should be made: • Example for how to produce a loud noise – e.g. bursting a balloon or banging wooden blocks together. • Time and distance measured. • Suitable equipment chosen to measure these. • Calculate speed using equation speed = distance/time • Allowance for distance sound travels = 2 × distance of person from wall / reflecting surface • Do repeats and calculate a mean.

- Reference to problems with reaction time with measurements.
- Improve method by either changing equipment e.g. using microphones to automatically detect the sound, or by improving reaction time issue (e.g. averaging multiple times).

7. a Count number of waves produced in set time (e.g. 1 minute), [1 mark] **or** divide number of waves produced in one minute by 60 [2 marks]

   b Waves constantly moving, [1 mark] alternative offered e.g. take photo of waves with a ruler next to it. [1 mark]

   c Describe a calculation from wavelength and frequency instead of a measurement [1 mark only] **or** measure time it takes for a wave to travel a set distance (e.g. length of ripple tank) [1 mark] calculate distance/time to work out speed. [1 mark]

Refraction of waves

1. Within block: straight line at smaller angle to normal than angle of incidence, [1 mark] ray leaving block: straight line at larger angle to normal than angle of incidence, [1 mark] exiting ray parallel to original ray. [1 mark]

2. a Minimum 2 wave fronts shown: wave fronts entering block change direction so bend towards normal, [1 mark] wave fronts closer together, [1 mark] wave fronts leaving block change direction to bend away from normal, [1 mark] unchanged wavelength (by eye) compared to original wave fronts. [1 mark]

   b Change of speed when a wave travels from one medium to a different medium. [1 mark]

The electromagnetic spectrum

1. transverse, frequencies, highest, lowest [1 mark each]

2. speed [1 mark]

3. a X-rays / gamma rays [1 mark]

   b Radio waves [1 mark]

   c Red [1 mark]

4. Speed is constant [1 mark] so to keep speed constant, the higher the wavelength the lower the frequency. [1 mark]

5. Frequency = wave speed/wavelength, [1 mark] 300 000 000/0.000 000 01 [1 mark] = 3×10^{16} Hz [1 mark]

Investigating infrared radiation

1. a Matt black [1 mark]

   b Thermometer [1 mark]

   c Any **one** of: infrared sensor has better resolution, better thermal contact, removes random reading / measurement error, records data automatically [1 mark]

2. Infrared radiation has a shorter wavelength than visible light. [1 mark]

Uses and hazards of the electromagnetic spectrum

1. Radio waves: television and radio

Microwaves: Satellite communications, cooking food

Infrared: electric heaters, cooking food, night-vision cameras

Visible light: fibre optic communications

Ultraviolet: energy efficient lamps, sun tanning

X-rays and gamma rays: medical imaging and treatments [1 mark each]

2. Absorbed by bone [1 mark]

3. Ultraviolet [1 mark]

4. Infrared [1 mark]

5. UV, X-rays and gamma, [1 mark] most ionising [1 mark]

6. a Wavelength (accept frequency) [1 mark]

   b Absorbed (by the atmosphere) [1 mark]

7. a Microwaves not refracted / reflected by ionosphere but radio waves are. [1 mark] (Accept microwaves can pass through ionosphere but radio waves cannot, unless transmitted at very large angle of incidence.)

   b Smoke absorbs visible light, [1 mark] infrared is transmitted through / not absorbed by smoke. [1 mark]

8. a 100 mSv [1 mark]

   b No, because a single X-ray is well below safe radiation dose for 5 years. [1 mark]

c 100/1.5 [1 mark] = 66 [1 mark] If they do several a day they may exceed that limit over 5 years. [1 mark]

d Leave room that X-ray machine is in whilst image is taken. [1 mark]

9. Gamma rays are emitted from the nucleus of an atom. [1 mark]

 Gamma rays are ionising radiation. [1 mark]

10. Gamma rays are (very) penetrating/can pass through the human body. [1 mark]

 Gamma rays can be detected (by a gamma camera). [1 mark]

Radio waves

1. Radio / TV broadcasting, [1 mark] communications network [1 mark] (do **not** accept satellite communications)

2. low, low, longer [1 mark each]

3. Oscillating / changing current (in electric circuit), [1 mark] produces electromagnetic wave. [1 mark]

4. Radio waves absorbed, [1 mark] causes charges in receiver circuit to oscillate / creates an alternating current. [1 mark]

5. Frequency [1 mark]

Section 7: Magnetism and electromagnetism

Magnets and magnetic forces

1. repel [1 mark] attract [1 mark]

2. Nickel [1 mark] Cobalt [1 mark]

3. Near poles [1 mark] (accept closest to magnet)

4. Non-contact [1 mark] Force acts between two magnets or a magnet and a magnetic material without them needing to touch. [1 mark]

5. Permanent magnet has its own field, [1 mark] induced magnet only becomes magnetic when in a magnetic field, [1 mark] induced magnet loses magnetism when removed from field, [1 mark] induced magnet attracted to either pole of permanent magnet. [1 mark]

Magnetic fields

1. Region around magnet in which a force acts on other magnets and magnetic materials. [1 mark]

2. Steel, [1 mark] The south pole of another magnet [1 mark]

3. A pole, [1 mark] this is where field lines are closest together and force is strongest. [1 mark]

4. South [1 mark]

5. Magnetic field of Earth weaker than field close to the permanent magnet, [1 mark] direction of field around permanent magnet at that point different to direction of Earth's magnetic field. [1 mark]

6. Place compass near magnet, mark dot / cross on paper / card where compass is pointing, [1 mark] after several repeats a line is drawn to join dots, [1 mark] add arrows on lines in direction compass needle points. [1 mark]

The magnetic effect of a current

1. Connect battery to either end of wire, [1 mark] start with compass far from wire, [1 mark] then show its change of direction as it gets closer to wire. [1 mark] Also accept place compass near wire, [1 mark] check direction of compass for no current, [1 mark] connect battery to wire and see if needle changes direction. [1 mark]

2. **a** Circular field – minimum of two concentric circles, not crossing [1 mark] all arrows shown on lines are pointing in a clockwise direction. [1 mark]

 b Larger current, [1 mark] shape wire into a coil. [1 mark]

 c Reverses [1 mark]

3. **a** (Soft) iron [1 mark]

 b Field pattern outside coil similar to field of bar magnet, [1 mark] minimum of 4 field lines, no field lines crossing, evenly spaced straight lines inside coil, [1 mark] correct direction of arrows from N pole to S pole [1 mark] (no mark if direction of any arrows contradict).

4. Current supply shown [1 mark] coil shown [1 mark] and iron core. [1 mark]

5. Place the (plotting) compass on the card and mark the position of the tip of the compass needle. [1 mark]

Move the compass on the card so the opposite end is at this position and mark the new position of the tip of the compass needle. [1 mark]

Repeat several times then draw field lines to link the marks made. [1 mark]

Add arrows on the field lines in the direction from N to S. [1 mark]

Fleming's left-hand rule

1. a Conductor moves [1 mark]

   b Conductor carrying current produces magnetic field (around wire), [1 mark] the two magnetic fields interact to produce force on conductor. [1 mark]

   c Motor effect [1 mark] (accept catapult effect)

2. a Arrow points away from centre of magnet / switch at right angles to both current and uniform field. [1 mark]

   b Stronger field [1 mark] higher current (accept increase p.d.) [1 mark]

3. $0.003 \times 0.5 \times 2$ [1 mark] $= 0.003$ N [1 mark]

4. $0.5/(0.1 \times 0.1)$ [1 mark] $= 50$ T [1 mark]

Electric motors

1. a From N pole to S pole (left to right) [1 mark]

   b Up [1 mark]

   c Down [1 mark]

   d Clockwise [1 mark]

   e Forces (on each side of coil) must reverse in direction. [1 mark]

   f Current is reversed [1 mark] using split-ring commutator (to reverse current direction every half turn). [1 mark]

   g Higher current, [1 mark] stronger field of permanent magnet, [1 mark] more turns on coil. [1 mark]